TINY BRITAIN

AA

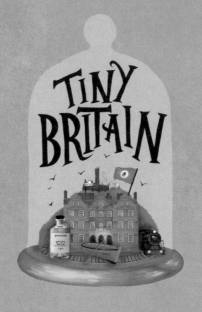

TINY BRITAIN

Dixe Wills

Published by AA Publishing, a trading name of AA Media Limited, Fanum House, Basing View, Basingstoke, Hampshire, RG21 4EA, UK.

First published in 2018
10 9 8 7 6 5 4 3 2 1

A CIP catalogue record for this book is available from the British Library.

ISBN: 978-0-7495-7922-7

Editor: Donna Wood
Art Director: James Tims
Designer: Tom Whitlock
Image retouching and internal repro: Ian Little

Printed and bound in the UK by Bell & Bain Ltd, Glasgow

A05573

theAA.com

To George Maurice Dixé
(1890–1916)

~ Contents ~

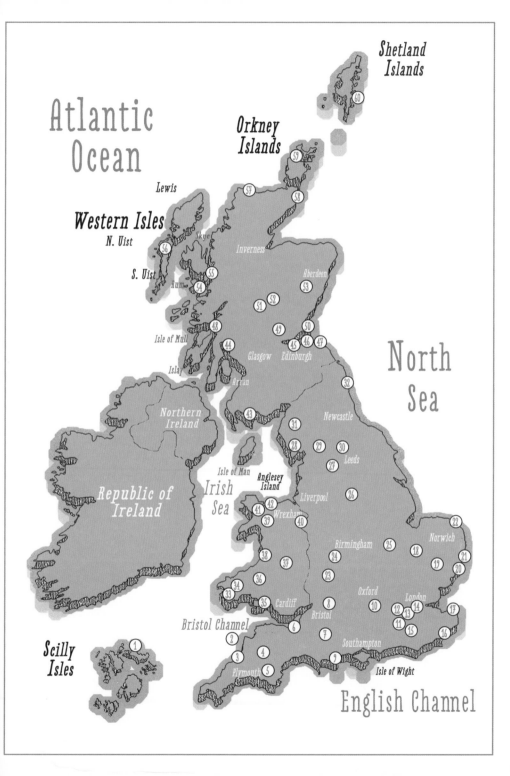

Introduction

It was the Greek/Phoenician philosopher Zeno of Citium who declared: 'Well-being is attained by little and little, and nevertheless is no little thing itself.' The great Stoic thinker was clearly on to something. Had he thought about it a bit more, he might have further deduced that well-being may also be achieved by focusing on little things. All too often, treasures that could enrich our lives are overlooked or disregarded simply because they are small and, by what goes for wisdom in the current age, therefore somehow unworthy of our attention.

It's my contention that that's a great loss. This book is thus an attempt to redress the balance – at least when it comes to tiny things in Britain. It's a celebration of the neglected, the ignored and the passed over in which I've attempted to explore their secrets, their stories, their idiosyncrasies and whatever else makes them special.

Tiny disregarded entities come in all manner of categories and so I've done my best to

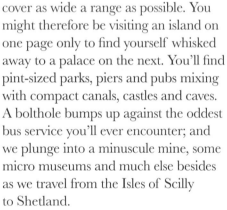

cover as wide a range as possible. You might therefore be visiting an island on one page only to find yourself whisked away to a palace on the next. You'll find pint-sized parks, piers and pubs mixing with compact canals, castles and caves. A bolthole bumps up against the oddest bus service you'll ever encounter; and we plunge into a minuscule mine, some micro museums and much else besides as we travel from the Isles of Scilly to Shetland.

Who knew that the shortest branch line in Europe (page 126) was served 214 times a day by trains that look like buses? Or that a theatre (page 122) based in a former gentlemen's toilet could provide such uplifting entertainment?

Why do World War II midget submarines (page 240) find themselves emerging from the sea twice a day on a Scottish beach? Who can solve the

mystery of the 17 diminutive coffins (page 235) discovered by a group of small boys on Arthur's Seat? How did a minute camera obscura in a replica Neolithic tumulus (page 294) come to appear on a remote Scottish island? And where exactly will a walk along the nation's shortest 'long-distance' footpath (page 208) take you?

If the underdog, the dark horse and the apparently insignificant are your kind of thing, I'll stick my neck out and say I think you'll enjoy *Tiny Britain* and will have a lot of fun visiting the entries in this book. If they're something you've never really paused to consider up until now, you're in for a real treat.

A timely treat, as it turns out. Quite by accident, this book is being published at a time when Great Britain is intent on reducing itself to Tiny Britain in as short a time as is possible. When the nation's name is officially changed, remember that you read it here first.

Dixe Wills
March 2018

England

Tiny Island
Teän, Cornwall

Once upon a time, a large chunk of land called Ennor broke off from the tip of Cornwall and made its way out into the Atlantic. By the time the Romans visited the island, it was nearly 30 miles from the coast. Then sometime in the early Middle Ages, rising sea levels flooded across the isle, submerging its valleys and breaking Ennor into the archipelago we know today as the Isles of Scilly.

One of the islands at the northern end of that archipelago is called Teän, a place-name that claims the rare distinction in Britain of possessing a diaeresis. Wedged between the islands of St Helen's on one side and the much larger St Martin's on the other, this roughly 40-acre piece of land is shaped a little like the Eagle landing craft of the Apollo 11 mission, with irregular jets of flame coming out at the bottom. It has just enough room for two small hills, both granite tors. The larger one is significant enough to have been given a name (the rather uninspired 'Great Hill'). Together they lord it over a mostly low-lying isle awash with gravel and erratics left over from glacial action that took place many eons ago.

The Great Hill may only rise just over 100ft out of the water but those who climb to the top are afforded one of the classic views of the Isles of Scilly. St Martin's immediately opposite, Tresco to the southwest and, across the shallow bowl of water flooded all those years ago, the main island of St Mary's to the south. Down below, Teän is ringed with little sandy bays or 'porths', the two most significant being West Porth and East Porth, which very nearly join up

together. Between these two, on the western edge of East Porth, stand the ruins of a chapel.

Teän is uninhabited nowadays but, as those ruins suggest, that was not always the case. There is evidence on the island to show that it has been lived on from the time before the great flooding of Ennor right up to the 19th century, albeit not continuously. The earliest indications of occupation come in the form of Bronze Age entrance graves that can be seen on both Great Hill and a spur of rock called Old Man in the southwest of the island. Brooches made in the Roman style have been found in the latter. At extremely low tides, the field boundaries laid out by farmers from the early centuries of the first millennium can be discerned.

It may seem unlikely looking at the Isles of Scilly now, but their history is littered with periods in which the islanders, particularly those on the smaller islands, were wracked with poverty and, at times, starvation. It's therefore no surprise to find that one official survey of the islands in the mid-17th century found Teän inhabited by just one man who had either taken to living in a ruined cottage or whose cottage had fallen into ruin around him.

The burning of kelp (a type of seaweed) provided an income of sorts to poorer islanders, and there's evidence that the practice was carried out on Teän too, apparently begun by a Mr Nance sometime in the second half of the 17th century. Burning kelp is a way of making sodium carbonate, a substance used in the manufacture of glass. Unfortunately, it's a very inefficient way of producing it, so you need a huge amount of kelp to produce a very small amount of sodium carbonate. Nevertheless, Nance and his descendants kept at it on Teän, eking out a living. At one time there were 10 of them living there in who knows what cramped conditions and state of penury. Certainly, the island lay abandoned again by the mid-18th century, though someone was heading over from time to time to oversee a crop of corn.

> One official survey of the islands in the mid-17th century found Teän was inhabited by just one man

Brave souls occasionally attempted to make Teän their home during the 19th century and livestock was still being taken over to Teän to graze as World War II was coming to a close, but the island has been unoccupied for over a hundred years now. Hedges (the Scilly name for walls) and the ruins of houses can still be made out but it would seem unlikely that new ones will ever be built there again.

The most interesting remains are those of the chapel. It has not been dated with any accuracy but is believed to have been built in the early Middle Ages, probably replacing an earlier wooden structure. It was almost certainly dedicated to Theona, which would explain the (somewhat corrupted) name of the island. Pope Celestine III mentions an isle called St Theona in the Scilly group in a papal bull of 1193, and it seems reasonable to suppose that this is the one he meant.

About the saint herself, little is known. In case you were wondering, she's not the St Theona who lived in Alexandria in the 4th century. Rather, it seems most likely that she was a hermit who came to live on the island, much as St Elidius did on neighbouring St Helen's, and was venerated after her death. A team of archaeologists organised a dig at the church in the 1950s in a bid to answer some of the questions surrounding the ruin. Much to their surprise, they discovered 16 graves in a cemetery crossed by the chapel's east wall. These were of much earlier date than the chapel and it has been speculated that the bones of an elderly woman found there are those of Theona herself.

But it would be completely wrong to think of Teän as devoid of life. Although the birdlife here is not what it once was – until quite recently puffins, herring gulls, lesser black-backed gulls, greater black-backed gulls and kittiwakes all bred on the island – there are still plenty of avian visitors from other islands.

Underfoot, there are the dainty petals of dwarf pansy and orange bird's-foot to enjoy, two plants found only on Scilly and the Channel Islands. They have been declining in numbers in recent years but the Isles of Scilly Wildlife Trust, which manages Teän, has been mimicking the grazing that once enabled these species to thrive by cutting the vegetation very short with brush-cutters. There are other rarities too such as saltwort and shore dock – one of

Europe's endangered endemic vascular plants, no less.

And be careful where you're putting your feet because you wouldn't want to step on a red barbed ant. It is close to extinction in Britain, there being just a single known nest on the mainland, somewhere in Surrey (its exact location is kept a secret in order to protect it).

However, the ant has been recorded in recent years on four islands on Scilly, including Teän, so anyone visiting should take special care not to disturb the insect in any way, should it still be clinging on to life there.

There are no scheduled boat services that land at Teän, which makes it more of a challenge to get to than a lot of islands in Scilly but it does have the advantage of assuring its tranquillity. It's possible to charter a motorboat to drop you off and pick you up later.

However, there is a much more pleasing way of making it to Teän. Simply hire a kayak, rowing boat, sailing boat or paddleboard from one of the major islands (St Martin's is barely a couple of paddle strokes away) and arrive under your own steam (or the steam of the wind, if you will). It can make for an extremely satisfying day out, though do be sure to check weather forecasts and tide timetables first – you really don't want to risk becoming a 21st-century castaway.

Useful information

Isles of Scilly, Cornwall

Walk Scilly: This annual festival of walks takes place in April and customarily organises a trip to Teän for a guided walk with a local expert visitislesofscilly.com | 01720 424036

Isles of Scilly Wildlife Trust: More information on the wildlife management of Teän can be found at ios-wildlifetrust.org.uk

Getting there by public transport

Take the train to Penzance, then sail to St Mary's (the main island of the Isles of Scilly) on the *Scillonian III* (islesofscilly-travel.co.uk; 01736 334220) which operates from mid-March to early November.

There are no scheduled boat services that land at Teän. However, there are plenty of companies – based on St Mary's, Tresco and Bryher – where you can hire kayaks, rowing boats, sailing boats, motorboats and even paddleboards.

Failing that, you can readily charter a boat from any of the major islands. Pop into the very friendly Tourist Information Centre at Porthcressa Bank, Hugh Town on St Mary's and they'll be able to sort you out.

Alternatively, if you're happy just to be conveyed around Teän without stepping foot on the island, the St Mary's Boatsmen's Association runs a relatively inexpensive 90-minute 'Round Island Lighthouse' tour which includes Teän, along with several other isles (scillyboating.co.uk; 01720 423999).

Tiny Lighthouse
Lundy Lighthouses, Devon

Lundy is one of the natural wonders of Britain. And to remove any doubt about that, it was voted so by readers of the *Radio Times*, who are not the sort to jest about such matters. It's a long, thin confection – about 3½ miles from tip to tip but only around ¾ mile wide – and as such forms something of a large obstacle in the Bristol Channel, orientating itself roughly north–south in a hopelessly ambitious attempt to form a bridge between Wales and Devon.

Lundy is roughly 11 miles from the Devon coast and 25 miles from South Wales and has not a single island neighbour, so it's little wonder that this majestic isolation has spawned a history marked by lawlessness, piracy and a yearning for independence.

The island also possesses two rather lovely and extremely petite late-Victorian lighthouses. One can be found at the northern tip of the island while the other is located at the southeastern corner. Trinity House, an association that has been doing its best to keep those on the sea from harm since its formation in 1514, was responsible for putting up both in 1897.

They were built as a long overdue response to a catastrophe. Trinity House had established Lundy's first lighthouse in 1819 on the summit of Chapel Hill in the southwest of the island. Unusually, it had two lamps – the lower one showed a fixed beam while the upper one gave a rapid flashing light. Unfortunately, the latter was so rapid that to those out at sea it appeared to be another fixed light, and from 5 miles away the two beams merged, giving the impression of one very bright permanent light. In November 1828, this caused the sinking of a ship called *La Jeune Emma*. Caught in a pea-souper, the captain imagined that he could see the fixed light from Ushant when it was in fact the combined beam of the two Lundy lights and as a result he ran the vessel onto the rocks. Only six of the 19 people on board were saved.

The North Lighthouse is a lonely outpost, far from the great majority of the island's buildings, most of which huddle together at the southern end. The journey there along the road-cum-track that runs right along the length of Lundy's spine is one of the most remarkable walks you can take in England. The coast on both sides is never far away and there's the added attraction of possible encounters with puffins (Lundy means 'puffin island'), wild Soay sheep and Lundy ponies.

Lodged on a little plateau carved out at the edge of the cliffs, the bright white lighthouse is an understatement turned into a building. It's just 55ft high and barely seems to rise above the flat-roofed keeper's house beside it. The visitor's first view of it comes from higher ground and the subsequent foreshortening effect only serves to exaggerate the lighthouse's Lilliputian appearance. However,

> By the magic of modern technology, both lighthouses are now controlled from a room in faraway Essex

its light still packs a punch – which is what matters really. Its beam has an intensity of 16,154 candela which allows it to be seen up to 17 nautical miles away. It was fuelled by petroleum vapour until electrification in 1971, and there were keepers maintaining it until 1985 when automation was introduced. Six years later the light was converted to solar power.

Lundy South Lighthouse is even shorter – it's just 52ft high – and has a slightly weaker beam (13,000 candela covering up to 15 nautical miles). Its history mirrors that of the North Lighthouse in every respect aside from the fact that its conversion to solar power came three years later. Walk out to the southeastern corner of the island, past Lundy's castle, and once again the first glorious sight you'll have will be from on high.

Sadly, this light hasn't always proved completely effective. One night in 1906, not 10 years after the lighthouse came into service, a Royal Navy battleship called HMS *Montagu* was cruising at full steam in dense fog when she went aground near the southwestern tip of the island. With her hull stuck fast, a few members of the crew rowed ashore to raise the alarm and seek assistance. Something was clearly awry with *Montagu*'s navigation because the captain was convinced that his ship was lodged on the rocks at Hartland Point, 9½ nautical miles away on the Devon coast. Gripping torches and groping their way along in the darkness and the fog, the landing party walked the entire length of the island before coming across the North Lighthouse where the keeper put them right as to where they were. One suspects that was a conversation the lighthouseman recounted for listeners many a time for the price of a pint.

The Royal Navy's various salvage attempts all ended in failure and over the following 15 years HMS *Montagu* was scrapped where she sat – an ignominious end to a proud battleship. Her remains – including live ammunition – are still mouldering near Shutter Rock, making it a popular site for divers.

By the magic of modern technology, both lighthouses are now controlled from a room in faraway Essex. Trinity House has an office in the port town of Harwich from which the lighthouses can not only be operated but also monitored for potential deficiencies and problems. As working lights, there's no public access allowed but they can be enjoyed from the outside – by day for their architecture and the wonderful seascape beyond, and by night for the drama of a light flashing its beam out over the darkened waters.

However, there is one lighthouse on Lundy you *can* go inside. Since 1969 the island has been administered by the Landmark Trust (on behalf of the National Trust), which has converted the vast majority of Lundy's buildings into appealing and, in some cases, unusual holiday lets. For the whole lighthouse experience, you can book yourself a memorable stay in one of the keepers' cottages at the Old Light, the lighthouse whose innovative double beam was found so wanting. At 97ft high, the lighthouse rather dwarfs its two successors and while it was working it held the dubious record for having the highest base (a full 469ft above sea level) of any lighthouse in Britain. Unfortunately, that meant that its light was often swallowed up by fog, a problem that the two tiny lighthouses, built much closer to sea level, suffer to a much lesser degree. Though were he alive today, the captain of the HMS *Montagu* would doubtless greet that assertion with something of a wry smile.

Useful information

Lundy, Devon

Trinity House Charity: For information about the work of the Trinity House charity which operates these and many other lighthouses and lightships around the country, have a look at trinityhouse.co.uk

The Old Light: The two former lighthouse keepers' cottages on Lundy are available to rent (sleeping 4 and 5 respectively) landmarktrust.org.uk/lundyisland

Getting there by public transport

It's always something of an adventure getting to Lundy. Start by travelling to Barnstaple, the end of the extremely picturesque Tarka line from Exeter St Davids. From the station hop aboard the number 21 bus (stagecoachbus.com; 01392 427711), which takes just under an hour to arrive at Ilfracombe.

The MS *Oldenburg* (landmarktrust.org.uk/lundyisland) sails from the north Devon seaside resort three or four times a week, the voyage to Lundy usually taking under 2 hours. There are also less frequent additional sailings from Bideford. The South Lighthouse is at the southeastern end of the island, not far from where the *Oldenburg* puts in.

As its name suggests, the North Lighthouse is at the far northern tip of Lundy, and can be reached via the one main path that runs along the 3-mile spine of the island.

3

Tiny Bolthole
Hawker's Hut, Cornwall

Everyone needs a little place to escape to, an oasis of calm where they can slough off the stresses and strains of modern life. It might be a favourite hilltop, a tranquil stretch of river bank or perhaps just a quiet park bench. For Robert Stephen Hawker – Anglican priest, antiquary and poet – it was the clifftops near his vicarage at Morwenstow in north Cornwall.

So soothing and yet stimulating did he find the scene that he cobbled together enough driftwood to fashion his own little den there. What is remarkable is that, over 170 years later, his ramshackle construction built into the cliffside is still in situ (albeit with repairs having been made over the years). It stands ready to admit artistic souls seeking inspiration or to provide a simple shelter for those who might be taken unawares by a change in the weather.

Hawker's hideaway near the Devon border has become the smallest property on the National Trust's books but must possess one of the most sumptuous yet uncomplicated views enjoyed by any of them. On both sides of the hut, verdant cliffs slide gracefully towards the Atlantic before suddenly hurtling down to drop into the waves below.

The man who built the tiny cabin was born in Plymouth in 1803, the first of nine children. His father joined the church and left the family when Robert was just 10. By then, he already fancied himself something of a poet. There's no denying that he was talented too. If Hawker is known at all today it is for his poem 'The Song of the Western Men', which he wrote when he was a stripling 21.

He garnered a reputation as an eccentric, but in a stiff-necked Victorian society obsessed with propriety, that was not all that difficult to do. If nothing else, Hawker's life is a reminder that love can bloom in the most unlikely of couplings. He was married at 19 to a woman, Charlotte I'ans, who was 22 years his senior. She died in 1863 and the following year Hawker – by now aged 60 – married again. His second wife, Pauline Kuczynski, was just 20. The couple had three children together.

As a boy, he had built himself a cabin in a remote part of a wood in order to spend the daylight hours reading there. This yearning to escape to rustic hideaways continued throughout his life, so it can have come as no great surprise to his first wife, Charlotte, when he set about making a clifftop retreat near their rectory home in Morwenstow sometime around 1844. Indeed, she may have thought it overdue, since her husband had already been the vicar there for nearly a decade by then (and would be so until 1874, the year before his death).

Hawker burrowed into the cliffside to create a tiny cave at whose entrance he built a small porch, thereby forming enough space within to lounge in comfort. The turf-covered roof protects a slate floor, and the only furniture comes in the form of two wooden benches. The entrance is separated into two hatches like a stable door. That way, if the weather was bad, he could close the lower door against the elements but still see outside and have enough light by which to read or write. However, on sunny days he could swing both doors wide, lean back against the far end of his little cabin and enjoy a practically unadulterated view of the sea and the sky. To look out over the two, safe in this little cocoon in the cliffs, is a gloriously enveloping experience that might lift or calm anyone's spirit. It was here that Hawker would pass hours on end writing poetry and casually smoking opium, like you do when you're a vicar.

There are two elements that combine to remind the visitor that

It was here that Hawker would pass hours on end writing poetry and casually smoking opium

all is not always so blissful in the world. The first is the emergence from the sea at low tide of some rather fearsome rocks.

The second is the hut itself: when you enter you are surrounded by physical evidence of the dangers facing those who sailed around this coastline. The wood that Hawker used to create his hut was not just any old driftwood but flotsam from three separate shipwrecks – the *Phoenix*, the *Alonzo* and the *Caledonia*. All three sank in 1843, resulting in dreadful loss of life.

The *Phoenix* went down with all hands in January near Hippa Rock, just a little to the south of the hut. The *Alonzo* foundered off the same stretch of coast in October. The crew was able to scramble into the ship's boat but it capsized, casting them all into the boiling sea to drown. The

Caledonia was a brig carrying wheat to Gloucester which hit the rocks in a September gale just below the hut at Higher Sharpnose Point (renamed 'Shark's-nose Head' in Hawker's 'The Smuggler's Song'). You can visit the graves of the crew in the churchyard at Morwenstow, where a replica of the ship's sword-bearing figurehead marks the last resting place of five of the sailors. All were buried by Hawker, who was particularly solicitous towards those in peril at sea.

Unusually for his time, he insisted that shipwrecked sailors be given a decent funeral in a churchyard, rather than being merely buried wherever they washed up. His tenderness extended to the survivors too. The sole mariner from the *Caledonia* who managed to reach shore, Edward Le Dain, was picked up half-dead by

a local farmer and taken to Hawker at the rectory. The vicar arranged for Le Dain to be cared for until he was back to full health. Eleven years later, when the sailor fathered a son, he named him Edward Robert Hawker Le Dain. The reverend and his wife became godparents to the child.

Visitors to the hut are following in celebrated footsteps. Hawker had many literary friends who came to see him in Morwenstow and he would take them on the rounds of the parish, an excursion that included the hut. Both Alfred, Lord Tennyson and Charles Kingsley (of *Westward Ho!* and *The Water-Babies* fame) have paid homage here. So when you visit, do make sure to bring along a pen and a notebook because you might just find yourself inspired to write the next Big Thing in poetry. Probably a good idea to leave the opium at home though.

Useful information

Near Morwenstow, Cornwall EX23 9SR (this postcode will take you to the centre of Morwenstow)

Always open | Admission free | nationaltrust.org.uk | 01208 863046

Getting there by public transport

North Cornwall is not entirely blessed with speedy transport connections. However, it is possible to reach Morwenstow without too many tears.

First you must get yourself to Barnstaple railway station, the terminus of the delightful Tarka line that runs across Devon from Exeter St Davids. From the station, hop on a number 319 bus (stagecoachbus.com; 01392 427711) to the charming village of Hartland, which takes about an hour. From Hartland a 217 bus (also Stagecoach) will convey you to Morwenstow in about half an hour.

From the Rectory Farm tearooms, take the track at the far end of the car park and follow the signs to the South West Coast Path. Once you reach the cliffs, turn left along the National Trail and look out for the signs to Hawker's Hut, which is very close to the path. In all, it's an invigorating walk of about a mile.

Tiny Bus Service
The Tavistock Country Bus, Devon

It's a cliché repeated almost to evisceration that we are all doomed to wait for a bus only for two (or, hey, perhaps even three) to turn up at the same time. However, there is a corner of Devon where there is absolutely no chance of this happening. Indeed, there's even a chance that, should you miss one particular bus, the next won't be along for another nine months.

The 112 route from Tavistock to Dawlish, operated by Tavistock Country Bus (TCB), has the distinction of being the nation's least frequent scheduled bus service.

There's something wonderfully Alice through the Looking-Glass about the timetable: the bus (or, to be more precise, the minibus) runs only on the fifth Saturday of the month, assuming there is one, and only once in each direction, and then only from April to September (it used to run from March to October but that was clearly deemed a bit extravagant). It means that the 112 will make the 1hr 46min trip a maximum of three times a year and sometimes just twice if the calendar is against it.

However unlikely it might seem, there is a perfectly reasonable rationale behind what appears to be mere caprice. Tavistock Country Bus, which was founded in 1981, is staffed entirely by volunteers. During the week, the operation takes care of all the local services in Tavistock, but on Saturdays, for a portion of the year, it throws its net somewhat wider, taking passengers as far as the bright lights of Exeter, Barnstaple, Torquay and even distant Truro. There's a service scheduled to each of these destinations on one of the

first four Saturdays of every month, which means they're guaranteed to run (with lucky Exeter and Truro getting visited every month from March to December). Dawlish, being the poor relation to these fleshpots of the southwest, has been accorded the fifth-Saturday slot. As company chairman and driver Douglas

Humphrey explains, 'It's not as popular as the other four places we run to.'

It's a terrible shame that that's the case because the 112's route is a glorious one that puts it on a par with any of the more renowned scenic bus journeys in Britain. Should you turn up at Parkwood Road in Tavistock

for the 9.05am bus (or, if you're not a completer-finisher, the brand new bus stop at Bedford Square in the centre of town three minutes later), you'll be in for quite a treat.

The minibus has room for 16 passengers but it's rarely filled to capacity so you should manage to get a seat (certainly, it would be quite a blow if you had to wait for the next one).

Tavistock itself makes for a grand port of departure. It's an ancient stannary (tin-mining) town with some very agreeable architecture in green stone. Take a look at the buildings as the bus makes its way out of town because you may well be looking at bits of Tavistock Abbey. A great deal of the stone from the abbey's buildings was spirited away to be put to domestic use when Henry VIII dissolved the monastery in 1538. In fact, so much was taken that if you visit the abbey today, all you'll see is the refectory, a porch and a couple of gateways.

Heading southeast out of Tavistock, the bus slips through the once important village of Horrabridge and the larger Yelverton before hauling itself up onto Dartmoor, passing close to Sheeps Tor and Piskie's Cave (see page 34). Beetling across Walkhampton Common, the first stop on the moor is Princetown, the closest Devon gets to a Wild West town and best known for being home to Dartmoor Prison, which, of course, played a key role in Sir Arthur Conan Doyle's *The Hound of the Baskervilles*. If the weather is good, the views you'll be fortunate enough to take in as you cross the moor, through Two Bridges and Dartmeet, are exceptional.

All subsequent stops to Tavistock are by request, so do be sure to apprise the driver of your plans should you be going all the way

Dropping down off Dartmoor, your volunteer driver guides you safely into Ashburton, a town hoary enough to have featured in the Domesday Book but still young enough at heart to have been the first town in Britain to elect an Official Monster Raving Loony Party councillor, later elevating him to the post of mayor. Next up comes the market town of Newton Abbot, birthplace of sports presenter David Vine and home for many years to Katy the Kickboxer. Before long, you've hit the sea at Teignmouth, from where it's a brief coastal drive along to Dawlish.

Nowadays, the former fishing port is a rather genteel seaside resort with some cracking sandy beaches, a better-than-average smattering of quality tearooms and a flock of black swans that were brought over from Uganda and live on a sanctuary called Dawlish Water in the middle of town.

The return service leaves promptly at 3.30pm, having given passengers nearly five hours to pootle around and commune with a swan or two.

The bus is only scheduled to return as far as Manor Garage, just beyond Yelverton. All subsequent stops to Tavistock are by request, so do be sure to apprise the driver of your plans should you be going all the way. If at any point you find yourself in need of a topic of conversation with your fellow passengers, you could ask them if they know anything about the controversial number change to the service. For many years this route was served by a 113 bus. The number was changed and TBC no longer runs a 113 bus to anywhere. The universe is full of mystery.

Useful information

Bus 112, Tavistock to Dawlish
tavistockcountrybus.co.uk | 07580 260683

Getting there by public transport

The bus begins its journey in Parkwood Road, Tavistock (9.05am), calling at Bedford Square (9.08) and the town's bus station (9.10).

The simplest method of making sure you catch it is to travel to Plymouth railway station, on the line from London Paddington to Penzance, and walk to North Hill, at the junction with Skardon Place, where you can pick up the number 1 bus (stagecoachbus.com; 01392 427711) at 7.43am (arrives Tavistock bus station 8.35) or 7.58 (arrives 8.50). The following bus (8.13) arrives at 09.05, which may be cutting it a little fine.

NB As mentioned above, the 112 bus runs only when there is a fifth Saturday in the month from April to September, so do consult a calendar before you leave the house.

5

Tiny Cave
Piskie's Cave, Devon

While Orkney may have its Finfolk (see page 307) and the Isle of Man its fairies, on Dartmoor it's all about pixies. 'Piskies', as they are known in the Devon dialect, are not evil characters as such but more mischievous spirits who, at the very worst, will abduct a baby, but that's where they draw the line. Their favourite trick is leading people astray on the moor.

This habit is so common that it even has a name: those who are walking across Dartmoor and suddenly find themselves unaccountably disorientated or perhaps lost on a route they've followed hundreds of times before are being 'pixie-led'.

This is no idle fairy tale told to children but a notion that is still believed or half-believed 'just in case' today. Not long ago, the superstition was so strong that it was tantamount to a religion. In 1890, William Crossing, without doubt the greatest ever authority on Dartmoor, wrote a seminal work on the region's little folk called *Tales of the Dartmoor Pixies*. In

it, he observed that the belief in the pixies' power to befuddle:

seems to be the one which has longest continued to keep a hold upon the country people. There are many now in our villages, who while they would not admit that they believed in piskies' doings, yet are full of instances of folks having missed their way in the most mysterious manner, and are more ready to incline to the idea that supernatural agencies were at work, than to seek the actual causes of the mishaps.

Of course, any self-respecting supernatural being must have a place to live. What could be more natural than that pixies, who are very diminutive and elusive creatures, should choose to live in a small hard-to-find cave off the beaten track?

The cavernette they chose is on the side of a hill called Sheeps Tor that rises above the tiny village of Sheepstor on the western side of Dartmoor. Despite appearances, the names probably have nothing to do with sheep but are more likely a corruption of the Old English scyttel, which means a bolt or a bar – more or less the shape of the outcropping granite on the tor. At about 1,200ft, it's not a particularly high peak but it still secures a wonderful view down to Burrator Reservoir for those who climb it in fine weather. Why the area near the summit is called Feather Bed is a mystery though, as anyone attempting to sleep the night on the rugged ground up there would no doubt concur.

The naturally formed cave hidden on the tor's southern flank actually goes by several other names, including Piskie's Grott, Piskie's House (the designation preferred by the Ordnance Survey) and Elford's Cave (more on that in a moment). However it's known, like many a thing worth discovering, Piskie's Cave does not give itself up without a struggle. Even when the pixies themselves aren't busily hiding it under a cloak of fog, mist or confusion, the cave's precise location among the clitter-clatter of rocks that strew the tor is not easily discerned. However, do not give up, because it's definitely there, whatever your senses might tell you. Also, you'll find a description to guide you in the information section on page 38.

As one might expect from a pixie cave, the entrance, a crevice between two upright rocks, is very narrow. It leads to a passage that continues for just a matter of a few feet before swinging sharply to the left and dropping a little. You now enter the cave proper. It's a rock-lined room with a low ceiling – you'll have to stoop – and is about 6ft long by 4ft wide. Its more or less regular walls

'Piskies', as they are known in the Devon dialect, are not evil characters as such but more mischievous spirits

do really give it the feeling of being a room rather than a rough space hewn in the hill as one might have expected. On your left is a rock that serves as a seat and in the far corner is a very low and slim passage. You may see the odd inscription on the rock within, as well as an offering or two to the pixies. It's a fantastically captivating space in which to find yourself – cut off from the outside world though only a few feet from it. And for those who (whisper it) refuse to believe in pixies, there's another story connected to the cave that makes it all the more beguiling.

Which brings us to the reason why it is also sometimes known as Elford's Cave. The fact that the cave is so tricky to find and yet is just about roomy enough for a person to inhabit without too much discomfort made it the perfect place for a hideout. That's certainly what John Elford – artist, member of parliament and disillusioned Roundhead – believed.

Elford was from nearby Longstone, where his family farmed and had an interest in tin (who doesn't?). He studied at Cambridge University and achieved sufficient renown with his paintings to become the earliest Dartmoor artist whose name we know. As a member of parliament he took part in the toppling of Charles I but sometime after the king's death in 1649 he became disenchanted with the Commonwealth and with Oliver Cromwell in particular. This falling out with his former comrades reached such a pitch that he involved himself in a plot to unseat Cromwell. When the plot was discovered, Elford became a wanted man.

In 1787, the Reverend Richard Polwhele, author of the three-volume tome *The History of Devonshire*, noted down what he had been told about the cave:

> *Here, I am informed, Elford used to hide himself from the search of Cromwell's party, to whom he was obnoxious. Hence he could command the whole country; and having some talents for painting he amused himself with that art on the walls of his cavern, which I have been told (says Mr. Yonge of Puslinch) by an elderly gentleman who had visited this place, was very fresh in his time.*

The hiding place proved a good one and Elford was never captured. Sadly, any paintings with which he might have adorned the walls of his little cell are no longer in evidence. However, a pair of his relief sculptures can still be seen inside the church at Sheepstor.

Since his time, Piskie's Cave has been left to the pixies, as is good and proper. An anonymous report in the 19th century claimed that the noise of them hammering metal or pounding apples to make cider sometimes emanated from the cave. The correspondent goes on to say that 'no one visits [the cave] without leaving a bunch of grass or one or two pins as a propitiatory offering to the mysterious beings who inhabit it'. It seems a small price to pay to ensure you get back down off Sheeps Tor without being pixie-led.

Useful information

Sheeps Tor, nr Sheepstor, Dartmoor, Devon
Always open | Admission free | NB Take a torch, a map and a compass

Getting there by public transport

This is not going to be easy. From Plymouth railway station it's a 10-minute walk to Skardon Place from where you can hop on a number 1 bus (stagecoachbus.com; 01392 427711) for the half-hour journey to Yelverton. That's as close as you'll get on public transport and you're still 3 miles away.

You can either walk – it's a hilly route on minor roads – or use Yelverton cab firms (Five Star; 07811 502430/Finch T R W; 01822 890224) who would get you to Sheepstor and pick you up after you've had your fill of the cave.

Walking out of Sheepstor with the church on your right, follow the road as it bends sharp right at a junction until it turns sharp left. At that corner take the bridleway on your right which heads up Sheepstor. At the point where it turns sharp left to follow the contour of the tor, leave the bridleway and head for a point just to the right of the summit of the tor. You should be able to pick up a rough path but the going is not spectacularly hard anyway. Piskie's Cave is on the slopes below a craggy cliff – Sheeps Tor's most prominent feature – and hidden among countless rocks. As a further help, from the entrance to the cave you should be able to see the roof – almost exactly side-on – of a large and prominent barn down below to the SSW. Failing that, try a grid reference. It's at roughly SX 566 680, assuming the pixies haven't hidden it.

Tiny Pier
Burnham-on-Sea Pier, Somerset

Nothing says 'British seaside' quite like a pier. And as an example of British understatement, Burnham-on-Sea's pier has no equal in the land, or indeed off it. It measures just 117ft, a distance Usain Bolt used to be able to cover in under 3.5 seconds when he really gave it a go. Furthermore, the minuscule structure is made to look even smaller by a vast expanse of sand and mudflats, a tiny stretch of which it spans.

The coastline in these parts experiences the second highest tidal range in the world, after the Bay of Fundy in Nova Scotia, and at low tide the sea retreats to a line a mile and a half away.

Britain's shortest pier provides a selection of little outlets selling refreshments and a larger café than might be expected in such a small space (it seats just over a hundred). It's very big on fish 'n' chips and pizza, but also serves less traditional pier fare such as panini and has a gluten-free menu so extensive as to be almost improbable. Ice cream, meanwhile, comes from milk extracted from cows living on a local farm.

For all that, the pier's true glory comes from its amusement arcade and bingo hall. The pavilion that houses them takes up about three-quarters of the entire pier, leaving just a little room on one side of it for those who would prefer to promenade outside and fill their lungs with good sea air.

But what is a pier without its High Temple of Gaudiness and Kitsch in which to fritter away small change as

if your job pays you rather too much if anything?

In short, it has all the essentials of a pier with the added bonus that it looks like a model of a proper one, which somehow adds an extra layer to the entertainment on offer.

It's all rather a far cry from the Burnham of old. Up until the end of the 18th century there was nothing here but a small fishing village, a place of little consequence on the edge of the Somerset Levels. It was only when townsfolk started to be attracted to the wide sandy beach by the mouth of the River Brue that the village began to expand and convert itself into a seaside resort.

The first pier to grace the town's seafront was much more ambitious than the present one and bore little resemblance to it. In 1858, the same year that Burnham got its first railway station, the Somerset Central Railway took it upon themselves to erect a stone pier that was 900ft long. Their aim was to run a steamer service that could whisk passengers straight off the brand new trains and across the Bristol Channel to Wales.

Unfortunately, although the service did get going two years later, it always struggled financially and closed in 1888. The pier was demolished.

The design of the current pier was inspired by the work of the great Isambard Kingdom Brunel at Bath Spa and Bristol Temple Meads railway stations. It was opened in 1914 and caused something of a sensation. This was not on account of the fact that it had taken three years to construct what was such a timid intrusion into the bay, but because it was the first pier in Europe to be built of reinforced concrete. Iron had been the preferred material of the Victorians, despite the obvious disadvantages inherent in putting a metal that corrodes into a wet and salty environment. Granite from Penryn in Cornwall was also used and continues to be used nowadays for running repairs. Given the exceptional tidal surges to which this

It measures just 117ft, a distance Usain Bolt used to cover in under 3.5 seconds when he really gave it a go stretch of coast is subjected – there were devastating floods as recently as 1981 that forced the subsequent building of an immense sea wall – it was initially feared that the pier would be swept away, but the reinforced concrete has proved up to the task thus far. There were plans to elongate the pier in its early days but nothing came of them. Perhaps it was felt that it might be pushing its luck a bit.

It's fair to say that the pier has had its ups and downs. Its nadir came in the 1960s, by which time the elegant pavilion was a dilapidated wreck. It was saved by Harry Parkin who bought the whole pier in 1968 and painstakingly restored the attraction, breathing new life into it. The pier has been operated by the Parkin family ever since. Sadly though, due to personal circumstances, they were forced to put it up for sale in 2016 and at the very end of 2017 it was announced that the pier had been snapped up by J Holland and Sons, a gaming company.

It must be acknowledged at this point that, technically, there does exist a more truncated pier in Britain. The Pier Bandstand in Weymouth, Dorset, has been shorter than Burnham's since 1986. However, it only achieved this feat because the council discovered that it would be 10 times cheaper to demolish virtually the whole 200ft-long structure than to repair it. They took to the task with unusual brio, holding a competition whose prize was the honour of pressing the button that would blow the pier to smithereens. When two lucky Birmingham schoolgirls did just that, they left a mere stump on which there was a rather lovely but suddenly lonely art deco building housing an amusement arcade (now a fancy Italian restaurant). To be honest, although it has the word 'pier' in its name, the Pier Bandstand is no more than a building that happens to be on stilts over a beach. There's no hint of a deck to walk on, which is the very least a pier should offer, so the title justifiably rests with Burnham.

In 2014, to mark the Somerset pier's centenary, the owners planned

to insert a pair of retractable roofs at the entrance so that the fun need not come to a halt when the weather turned less than clement. However, there was a bit of a hoo-ha with the council over whether the roofs were appropriate for the local area. As a consequence, they weren't installed until the following year. It means that, ironically, the nation's shortest pier may well possess the nation's longest retractable pier covering. One can only dream that some day we might live in a world where piers could compete for the glory of holding the official record for that sort of thing.

The roofs certainly come in for some use because, unlike many piers, the one at Burnham-on-Sea remains open all winter. Indeed, the owners make rather a virtue of the chillier weather. The café offers both mulled wine and mulled Somerset cider, both served to a recipe that includes star anise and bay leaves.

The added bonus of some spiced-up alcohol makes the pier worth visiting at any time of year. When you do though, just a word of caution: don't bother observing that, when it comes to short piers, Burnham has no peers – they've heard that one.

Useful information

The Esplanade, Burnham-on-Sea, Somerset TA8 1BG

Open daily except Christmas Day | Admission free

Getting there by public transport

From the Highbridge and Burnham-on-Sea railway station, on the Bristol to Taunton line, it's a 2-mile walk through Highbridge, left onto Burnham Road and left again onto Marine Drive, which leads right to the pier.

Alternatively, save your calories and walk the short distance from the station to the bus stop on Church Street at the corner of Newtown Road and pick up the 21 bus (firstgroup.com/somerset; 0345 602 0121) to the pier.

7

Tiny Castle
Nunney Castle, Somerset

By a brook on the edge of a village in Somerset, just to the east of the Mendip Hills, stands a little-known castle. The village of Nunney makes for a startlingly attractive setting for what is a real gem of a place. Amid lawns and graceful trees, with views of woods beyond, the compact and partially ruined stronghold is a very pleasing sight indeed. However, as you approach it, you'll begin to notice a few rather curious details.

In the case of the vast majority of moated castles, the moat is merely a water-filled ditch circling the walls. Nunney, on the other hand, looks more like a castle that has squeezed itself onto a tiny island in the middle of a large pond. The domestic appearance of the little lake turns out to be misleading – it is deep and steeply shelved. As it happened, on the occasion when the castle was attacked, the moat proved to be of little use, though that owes more to advances in the technology of ballistics than to any failings it may have had as a defensive barrier. (Nowadays it can be crossed via a simple wooden footbridge.)

The moat surrounds walls that, with one notable exception, are reasonably high. The structure as a whole though leaves one with the impression that it has been shrunk in the wash. It has a round tower at each of its four corners but at both ends the towers are built so close to each other that they're almost in danger of overlapping. Even the walls on the longer sides of the castle are of no great span.

Looking up, you'll see myriad stone supports poking out of the walls near the top. Once these would have cradled the stone parapet that ran all around the castle and from which it could have been defended. Now, however, they make the fortress look as though it has one side of a zip sticking out of it and that it's waiting patiently to be reunited with its other half. Rather than making it seem ridiculous, this foible merely adds to the building's charm.

Nunney Castle would probably not have existed at all had it not been for the Hundred Years' War, the 116-year on-and-off conflict between England and France that eventually ground to a halt in 1453. The local lord of the manor, Sir John de la Mare, went off to fight alongside Edward the Black Prince, King Edward III's oldest son. Sir John enjoyed a successful campaign during which he helped to capture various members of the French nobility for whom large ransoms were subsequently paid. Flush with this honourably acquired pelf, he petitioned the king for permission to crenellate his manor house at Nunney and implement other adaptations that would turn it into a castle.

In the event, de la Mare (sometimes spelled de la Mere) decided to build a whole new fortified manor house more or less next door to the one he already owned at the foot of a hillock. This 1373 construction was the first incarnation of Nunney Castle. It was not a building that had any pretensions to being a stronghold, but was more a statement about the sort of dwelling Sir John thought fit for a victorious knight back from the wars. The nobleman used the king's own architect and had the exceptionally generous moat dug (it was at least 10ft deep) after the manor house was completed. A mighty 12ft-high wall was constructed forming three sides of a good-sized bailey, with Nunney Brook acting as the fourth.

Come the 16th century the castle was given a sprucing up. It was purchased sometime after 1560 by a wealthy Londoner named Prater who made wholesale improvements. The floors and ceilings were ripped out and rebuilt at different levels, windows were enlarged, a splendid spiral staircase was installed, and the moat was pushed back a little from the walls, creating the attractive terrace that is still in evidence today.

But then came the only action Nunney Castle ever saw. Its brush with organised violence turned out to be calamitous. The fortress had been passed down the generations and in the 1640s was in the ownership of Richard Prater, a staunch Catholic and arch Royalist. The castle, which was garrisoned by Irish mercenaries, was besieged by Parliamentarian troops under Sir Thomas Fairfax in September 1645. The siege lasted just three days. On the third, the Roundheads fired a cannon from the top of the low hill that rises to the north of the castle. The cannonball blew a great hole in the northwest wall at the first-floor level and Prater surrendered the castle without further ado. Following Oliver Cromwell's orders, Fairfax had the roof ripped out and the floors taken apart so that the castle could not be re-occupied by Royalists (though Richard Prater's son George did manage to reclaim the building on the restoration of the monarchy in 1660). Many of the fixtures and fittings found their way into the homes of villagers in Nunney, and some cottages today still boast a fireplace, wooden beams or some artefact from the castle.

The great breach – that testament to Nunney Castle's brief yet unfortunate moment in the limelight – remained until Christmas Day 1910 when virtually the whole of the northwest wall collapsed. Almost as

With views of woods beyond, the compact and partially ruined stronghold is a very pleasing sight

soon as it had been slighted, the castle had become overgrown with ivy and choked with weeds and shrubs and undermined by the roots of trees that grew up around it. Even so, it became a tourist attraction in the late 19th century, with visitors paying a small fee to poke about in the ruins and undergrowth. Thankfully, no one appears to have been doing so when the disaster occurred.

The entire castle might have gone the same way as the northwest wall had it not been for the Ancient Monuments Consolidation and Amendment Act that came into force three years later. Nunney was given scheduled ancient monument status and work began in 1916 to ensure the preservation of the remainder of the castle. It proved quite a job and operations were still going on in the early 1930s.

The castle was bought at auction for £600 in 1950 by Robert Walker, a man who lived in the village and also happened to be heir to the Johnny Walker whisky fortune (and owned a Formula One team, as one does).

Although the castle is still in private hands, responsibility for its upkeep was transferred to the state in 1962. The castle is now cared for by English Heritage and is open to the public.

But that is not the end of the story for Nunney Castle. Every year, on the first Saturday in August, the somewhat unsuccessful miniature fortress gets a chance to shine. That's the day when the Nunney Community Association holds a daytime street market and fair in the village of Nunney. The castle plays its part by acting as a dramatic backdrop to the musical artistes who perform as part of the festivities.

Useful information

Castle Street, Nunney, Somerset BA11 4LW

Open any reasonable time during daylight hours | Admission free

english-heritage.org.uk

Getting there by public transport

Take yourself along the Bristol to Weymouth line to Frome railway station. From there make your way to the Market Place in the centre of town whence a 162 bus (tinyurl.com/y7zdn6y3; 01373 471474) will whisk you the 3½ miles to Nunney in 12 minutes.

Tiny Football Team
Forest Green Rovers/Ladies, Gloucestershire

Imagine settling down with your freshly purchased copy of *Roy of the Rovers*, still the comic *du choix* for football-obsessed boys and girls (who also happen to read comics). You open its pages and begin reading a story about a football team (called The Rovers, naturally) from a hamlet in an unfashionable part of the country.

The club has a long but undistinguished past, once even achieving the feat of completing a season with no points at all. However, the many decades of obscurity are put behind them as they begin to climb the non-league football ladder until they're punching well above their weight. They win a prestigious trophy (probably against a team of miners) and even beat a league side in the FA Cup (to make it plausible, let's say Rotherham United) but it seems like they have reached the pinnacle of their ambition.

Then a local businessman (with some improbable name like 'Dale Vince') takes over the club, institutes a new fitness regime untried at any football team in the land, and introduces some eccentric ideas such as making the grass on the pitch organic and having it cut by a robot lawnmower. The team does even better, reaching the play-offs to enter the football league, but their hopes are cruelly dashed when they crash to defeat in the semi-finals. The next year, they make the final of the play-offs, but once again the dream of being the first village team to play in the football league comes crashing down around their ears. Still, at least they got to play at Wembley. But these two near misses make it all the sweeter when, the following year, they win their semi-final, then go on to trounce a former giant (let's not go too mad – maybe settle for Tranmere Rovers) in the final to claim their spot in the football league at last. The last box of the comic strip is a close-up of the captain's face as he drinks champagne from a trophy and blithely breaks the fourth wall by aiming an insouciant wink at the reader. You chuckle, toss the comic on a nearby ottoman, and go back to your work as a clump-press minder or an adviser to the Home Office on public-facing systems design.

The story, of course, turns out not to be fiction at all but entirely true (as any Rotherham or Tranmere Rovers fan will confirm, with a wince). Forest Green Rovers, based in the tiny Gloucestershire town of Nailsworth (population 5,800), was formed in 1889 as 'Forest Green' by the Reverend E J H Peach. It was named after a hamlet that has since been subsumed into the town. The team knocked about in various minor leagues and county leagues (finishing with no points in one season because, although they had won one game, they had two points deducted for fielding an ineligible player). Eventually, they started climbing – first to the Hellenic League and then

to the Southern League, picking up the FA Vase along the way by winning the 1982 final against Rainworth Miners' Welfare. After a short period in which they were known as Stroud FC – taking the name from the nearest town of any size – they reverted to Forest Green Rovers and after several mediocre years finally made it to the Conference (now the National League) in 1998, putting them just one step away from playing in the 92-team football league.

The club was twice saved from relegation because other teams were demoted in their stead on technical or rule-breaking grounds before Dale Vince took a major shareholding in 2010 and became club chairman. He's the founder of the green electricity company Ecotricity, which has its headquarters up the road in Stroud.

Vince has made Forest Green Rovers the first vegan football team to play at such a high level in England. The organic pitch cut by a GPS-guided robot was also one of his innovations, as are the stadium's solar panels that generate 10% of the ground's electricity needs. After heartbreaks in two consecutive play-offs, Forest Green Rovers was promoted to Division 2 (that's Division 4 in old money) of the English Football League in 2017 by defeating Tranmere

Rovers 3–1 in the play-off final at Wembley. Nailsworth thus became the smallest town that has ever been represented in the football league.

The capacity of Forest Green Rovers' ground, the New Lawn, is around 5,000. This is not much less than the population of Nailsworth and several thousand more than that of Forest Green, which is surely also a record. However, time is running out for those who would see the pride of Forest Green playing in their home (former) hamlet. A move to a new and even more eco-friendly ground is on the cards. The proposed site for the stadium is the Eco Park complex, just to the west of the town of Stonehouse and around 8 miles northwest of Nailsworth. It's the work of the late Zaha Hadid, the world-famous Iraqi architect who designed Glasgow's Riverside Museum and the Aquatics Centre for the 2012 London Olympic Games. Constructed almost completely from wood, it will be a 5,000-seater stadium whose capacity can be doubled if the team continues its extraordinary rise. If it needs to be painted, the club is likely to save a bit of money because there's a tradition going back to the 1950s that the fans turn up voluntarily to paint their team's stadium.

Useful information

Men's team: The New Lawn, Another Way (see what they did there?), Nailsworth, Gloucestershire GL6 0FG (satnav users should put in GL6 0ET). Tickets can be bought in advance at a discount from the Forest Green Rovers website | Tickets purchased on match day: adult £18–£23, young adult (16–21) £9–£13, junior (U16) £6–£9, kid (U11) free–£4

forestgreenroversfc.com | 01453 834860 | Details of fixtures for the whole season can be found on the website.

Getting there by public transport

Naturally, you wouldn't suppose the football league's smallest club would be served by a railway station and you'd be right. Nailsworth is 4 miles south of Stroud, whose railway station is on the Golden Valley line between Gloucester and Swindon. From the station it's a short stroll to Stop M at Merrywalks, where a number 63 bus (stagecoachbus.com; 01452 418630) will whisk you to Forest Green and very close to the New Lawn stadium.

Perhaps it's something in the Nailsworth water, but it's not only the men's team that has massively overachieved. Forest Green Rovers Ladies have also been pulling up trees (or, more likely, planting them) in their much shorter history and have briefly climbed even higher than the men's team. Founded in 2002, they made short work of the South West Women's Football League, picked up a trophy, and in the 2007–08 season reached the fourth round of the FA Women's Cup, when their progress was halted only by the mighty Liverpool Ladies. They've even spent some time in the FA Women's Premier League Southern Division, the third tier of women's football in England, but now ply their trade in the fifth-tier South West Women's Football League Premier Division, playing their home games at nearby Slimbridge AFC's ground.

Together, the two teams have written what must be the greatest David/Davina versus Goliath tale in the history of English football. So look up a fixture list, head to south Gloucestershire, buy a green-and-black scarf at the stadium and cheer on the valiant lads or lasses. Win, lose or draw you'll be able to tell your grandchildren, 'Yes! I was there.'

Useful information

Ladies team: Slimbridge AFC, Thornhill Park, Wisloe Road, Cambridge, Gloucestershire GL2 7AF | tinyurl.com/ya2vdpou

Getting there by public transport

From Cam and Dursley station, on the line from Bristol to Birmingham, it's a 1½-mile walk. Strike out along Box Road to the main road, turn right and follow the footpath along the A4135, cross bridges over the railway and the M5 motorway and continue onwards to Wisloe Road and Slimbridge AFC's Thornhill Park ground.

Tiny Cinema
Bournemouth Colosseum, Dorset

Sadly, tiny cinemas tend to be ephemeral beasts. The 21-seat Screen Room in Nottingham, for instance, went dark in 2011 after just nine years. La Charrette, a converted railway carriage in a back garden in Gorseinon, was the exception that proved the rule by holding the record as the smallest cinema in Wales for over 50 years.

However, it too was finally shunted into the sidings in 2008 and is now preserved for posterity by the Gower Heritage Centre near Swansea. Meanwhile, other minuscule cinemas, like the Blue Walnut Café in Torquay, play host to a film club that meets only occasionally. The beautiful raked 23-seater on the Devon coast projects one film a month to a gathering of celluloid cognoscenti. So one can only hope that the Bournemouth Colosseum manages to buck the trend.

Furnished with just 19 seats, it is the UK's smallest cinema. Opened in September 2013 by Paul Whitehouse (not that Paul Whitehouse) in the premises of his Lavish Life art gallery, it makes watching a film a peculiarly intimate experience. The cinema is located in Westbourne, an area in the west of Bournemouth, and runs to a 96in screen and a state-of-the-art projector provided by a local television shop. The seating comes from a rather less obvious source, having first seen service in the Welsh National Assembly. For those who quail at the thought of sharing a space with even a dozen or so strangers, the cinema also offers a two-seat 'royal box' from which denizens may presumably show their appreciation for the film as the final credits roll by rattling their jewellery.

When the lights go down, the screen is most likely to be filled with classics from the 1950s to the 1970s, while every second Wednesday the schedule includes a film of a concert or a music documentary (or, as director Marty DiBergi would put it, a 'rockumentary'). The films are mainly selected on the basis of an ad hoc poll conducted in the gallery. Customers are asked to name their favourite films and those that are mentioned most frequently are the likeliest to get an airing. However, the cinema can also be hired for private screenings, so anyone can corral a group of like-minded friends and arrange a viewing of the director's cut of that Japanese art-house gothic-horror pastiche you missed first time round, or whatever else takes your fancy.

Unusually, the cinema also has a supper club twice a week, with a two-course meal tailored to the film being projected afterwards. This is all well and good, of course, if the moving picture in question is the kitchen-based animation *Ratatouille* or the crime thriller *Artichoke*, but you might want to think about fasting for a few days beforehand if the Colosseum ever shows *La Grande Bouffe (Blow-Out)*, the 1973 Marco Ferreri flick starring Marcello Mastroianni and Philippe Noiret in which four men go to a house in rural France with the express purpose of eating themselves to death.

But that is not all. Fired by the success of the cinema, Whitehouse has recently opened a second, even smaller space on the same premises. Screen 2 has just eight seats and official recognition as the new smallest permanent cinema in Britain is currently being sought from Guinness World Records.

Surprisingly, for a place the size of Bournemouth, there had been no cinema in the town since the 1970s, when the Grand was converted into a bingo hall, so the Colosseum's arrival was long overdue. And for those who attend particularly niche pub quizzes, the answer to the question 'Which was the first film ever shown in Britain's smallest cinema?' is Billy Wilder's Oscar-winning comedy *The Apartment*, a film whose main mise en scène was in itself appropriately bijou.

Useful information

Mon, Wed, Fri and Sat 7.30pm (entrance fee £7.50) | Supper club (£15 inc. film) Tue and Thu 7.30pm followed by film at 8.15pm | Annual membership fee £9.50 | bournemouthcolosseum.co.uk | 01202 769092

Getting there by public transport

Bournemouth railway station, on the line between London Waterloo and Weymouth, is about 2½ miles from the cinema. There are several buses that run from the station to Westbourne, with the M1 (morebus.co.uk; 01202 338420) stopping right outside Westbourne Arcade.

At Blue Walnut Café, Torquay, the Mickelodeon Film Club shows films on the third Thu of the month | bluewalnuttorquay.co.uk | 01803 394113

La Charrette is open to the public as a permanent exhibit at the Gower Heritage Centre in Parkmill, Gower, and is also available to hire for birthday parties and other events | gowerheritagecentre.co.uk 01792 371206

10

Tiny Town
Watlington, Oxfordshire

When does a village become a town? Is it a question of size? Population? Importance? Or simply perception? In the case of Watlington its designation as a town appears to be based entirely on ancient history.

The south Oxfordshire community was handed a royal grant to hold a market by Henry III in 1252, instantly converting it from a mere village to a market town. It's a status the 2,727 population of Watlington hold dear: woe betide the visitor who saunters in and lets slip the word 'village' in relation to the place. Furthermore, Watlington's claim to the title of England's Smallest Town is one its inhabitants will defend to the death. One can only hope there's never a showdown with the good citizens of Fordwich in Kent (see page 87) or the streets will run red with blood, or at the very least green with the ink of letters written to the local newspaper (albeit that Watlington doesn't actually have its own newspaper, though it does have a magazine called

the *Watlington Times* to keep tabs on the goings-on in the town).

Thankfully, there is no argument about Watlington's location: the town sits rather prettily on the edge of the Vale of Oxford. This places it at the foot of the Chiltern Hills, about 3 miles to the southwest of the M40. The Icknield Way passes close by, which was the Saxon equivalent of living near a motorway when the first settlement was established here sometime in the 6th century. It's a compact place, with its main shopping streets arrowing out in three directions from a small market square, in the middle of which sits a very fine 17th-century town hall.

Watlington's lack of growth over the centuries can be attributed in large measure to its distance from the nearest

river (the closest, the Thames, is six miles away). The difficulty in getting materials in and out of the town meant that no great manufacturing processes were established there in the medieval period. It then proceeded to be a spectator of the Industrial Revolution rather than an active participant. Even its Saturday market withered and in 1852 came to an end altogether.

The advantage of all this twiddling of thumbs while the march of progress happened elsewhere is that Watlington is now the repository of a great number of well-preserved historic buildings, mainly dating from the 16th century to Georgian times (with a Norman church thrown in for good measure). If you shut your eyes and ears to the traffic that passes along the town's main arteries, it is just about possible to imagine the place as it was when the local womenfolk strolled around in Brunswick gowns or, further back still, when news arrived of Drake's victory over the Spanish Armada.

Watlington's relative unimportance has also meant that it has remained off the radar of most corporate businesses and chain stores. As a result, its main streets are lined with a surprising number of independent specialist shops and locally owned eateries, which makes a welcome change from the dreary homogeneity that besets so many other urban centres in Britain.

History hasn't always passed the town by, of course. The tellers of the Domesday Book came calling in 1086 to tot up the worth of the farming community there (£610, apparently). Watlington was used by both Roundheads and Cavaliers as a base in the Civil War, with Cromwell himself setting out for a successful raid from the town in April 1645.

Puritanism of a slightly different vein revisited in the 19th century, when arch Methodist George Wilkinson bought up six of the town's many pubs and promptly closed them down (much to the delight of the remaining hostelries, one would imagine). The Chequers is probably the pick of Watlington's pubs today. Its genesis is obscure but it is likely to have been established in the 16th century. Its exterior certainly has the pleasing look of an inn that has seen rather too much.

The origins of the town hall are much better known. It was built in 1664–5 at the behest of one Thomas Stonor, with the upper room used as a boys' grammar school. An elegant brick building, it sits on an island at the meeting of three main roads. In a nod to the town's roots, a covered space on the ground floor is now home to a fruit and veg stall.

Exactly 100 years after construction work on the town hall commenced, Watlington's other great landmark – the Watlington White Mark – was created by a local squire called Edward Horne. The obelisk-like shape cut into the chalk on Watlington Hill appears at first sight to possess some sort of esoteric symbolism. The truth is at once more prosaic and rather odder. Horne had a fancy that the town's St Leonard's church would be improved if it had a spire. Rather than seek to build one, he had this 270ft-long spire shape cut into the hill so that, when viewing the church from his house, an optical illusion was created, giving the impression that the church had in fact been fitted with a spire.

Watlington's railway station seems to have been built on the same principle. No doubt mindful of Watlington's predilection for poor transport links, the Watlington and Princes Risborough Railway Company boldly laid a line out to the town in 1872 and gave the inhabitants the illusion of having a station by calling it 'Watlington' but placing it half a mile away in the hamlet of Pyrton. Despite the inconvenience, passenger services ran until 1957 when the station was closed. Sixty years later, the station building is still in evidence, albeit sadly derelict, and the track bed of the line it served is detectable only to those with a keen eye for such things.

Some visitors to Watlington might find themselves overcome with a feeling of déjà vu, marking them out as fans of *Midsomer Murders*, the popular television series about chocolate-box villages with homicide rates more apocalyptic than a Brazilian favela at the height of a gang war. Watlington has featured in no fewer than five episodes. The cameras have also followed Inspector Morse to the town in his bid to stop the mindless slaughter.

As with the Watlington White Mark, reality has proved rather stranger than fiction. For a short while in the 1980s, peaceful little Watlington gained a reputation as the drugs capital of southern England, and was even the subject of a television documentary about its unlikely status. Things have calmed down somewhat since those high old days and the town seems reasonably content to have settled back into its perennial role as an Oxfordshire backwater.

Finally, should you visit Watlington, don't forget to look up now and again. Red kites have been reintroduced to the area and can often be seen patrolling the skies above the town, as if somehow attempting to protect it from the predations of the 21st century.

Getting there by public transport

The major reason for Watlington's lack of growth – those poor transport links – continues to dog/bless the town today. There is a direct bus from Oxford (the T1, from St Aldates in the city centre; thames-travel.co.uk; 01865 785400) but it does not run all day (and very infrequently at weekends) and, at its speediest, takes the best part of an hour to cover the 15 miles that separate the university town and the market town. On the upside, that does at least give those arriving by bus time to prepare themselves mentally for the Watlington experience.

Tiny Pub
Platform 3, Surrey

Beyond the ability to serve up a decent round of drinks, what makes a fantastic pub? Is it the atmosphere? The volume of obsolete farm equipment nailed to the walls? The quality of banter supplied by the regulars parked around the bar? Whatever it is, Claygate's Platform 3 proves that mere lack of size is no barrier to greatness.

Britain's smallest pub operates out of a shed-sized station-side building whose interior dimensions are truly minuscule. It measures 9ft by 8ft and has just about enough space for three customers standing at the bar if they all agree to keep their elbows to themselves. It is true, as co-owner Alex will tell you, that the pub once appeared on regional television news for managing to squeeze 23 morris men into it, but that doesn't appear to be a frequent occurrence. The morris men do, however, turn up to dance outside the pub every Christmas. Tradition dictates that on Boxing Day each year they visit every pub in Claygate, starting with Platform 3.

The little brick-and-tile structure – designed to look like a model house – has been positively Whovian in its ability to regenerate itself. It began life as a coal-ordering office. In the days when coal fires were the norm, Claygatians would order however many sacks they required. The coal came in by train, was stacked behind the hut, and the coalman would deliver it to the door or deposit it into the customer's coal hole. When coal fires were phased out, the office closed and its journey into the wild world of transanimation began. It has been a minicab office (that's now next door), a second-hand bookshop, an estate agent and an interior design shop selling fabrics and other essential trappings of the suburban home. In August 2012, the incredibly friendly husband-and-wife proprietors Alex and Sue bought up a microbrewery and produced their first firkin the following year. Such was the success of the venture that they took over the bijou edifice next to Claygate station, transformed it into a pub, and opened to customers in June 2015.

That's not to say that Alex, a son of Claygate, is new to the game. Trained as a biochemist, he had been brewing at home for three decades before he and Sue took the plunge and became brewers-cum-publicans.

'I like to say my beers are balanced,' Alex declares. 'They have flavour and character at low gravities.'

He has come up with seven different beers from the couple's Brightwater Brewery so far: Daisy Gold, Village Green (brewed just once a year from fresh hops), All Citra, Top Notch, Wild Orchid (with added Madagascan vanilla pods), Lipsmacker and Little Nipper. They range in strength from All Citra's 4.3% ABV (alcohol by volume) to the session beer Little Nipper's 3.3%.

A selection of two or three are on tap at the pub at any one time (with an occasional guest beer), and all of

them are available either in bottles (in which the beer is vegan) or takeaway draught form, drawn off into a 2-pint container, 4-pint flagon or a mighty 5-litre (nearly 9-pint) mini-keg, depending on one's particular needs.

They're no ordinary beers either: both Daisy Gold (named after a well-behaved dog) and All Citra were awarded a much-prized gold star in the 2016 Great Taste Awards.

There is, of course, the usual range of wines and spirits one would expect at a pub as well. Those who prefer to imbibe a cider are not forgotten either: Brightwater produces a tipple called Claygate Cider, made mostly from a local russet dessert apple called the Claygate Pearmain which has been around since the days of Queen Victoria.

The pub is probably best described as cosy, rather than 'deceptively spacious', as the previous estate agent occupier might have put it. The short bar with its three taps is piled high with posh crisps; beer bottles and cans

Britain's smallest pub operates out of a shed-sized station-side building whose interior dimensions are truly minuscule

of soft drinks line the walls; a small fridge is packed with more bottles and cans; and a plastic hop plant serves as a fringe between walls and ceiling. Covering one gable end are press cuttings and awards (the pub has already scooped a barrel load in its short lifetime), while the ceiling has a growing collection of beer pump badges affixed to it.

Of course, that doesn't leave a great deal of room for patrons. Happily, accommodation has been made for the clientele around half a dozen tables set outside. These are illuminated by tea-light lanterns and, if inclement weather has been forecast, covered by a large gazebo affair. And if a surprise cloudburst should interrupt proceedings, customers simply pick up their drinks and take shelter under the station roof until the deluge is over.

For winter drinkers, Sue recommends a combination of 'duffel coats and bobble hats', and for those who have forgotten to bring their bobble hats, the pub sells its own branded ones (along with a whole host of other merchandise from tote bags to baseball caps). Only if the weather is absolutely foul does the pub close, though because of Claygate's propensity to suck up all of Britain's good weather, that doesn't happen all that often.

Clearly, the premises are too small to contain a kitchen, so there's no food available beyond the usual bar snacks and a few sweets for children. However, patrons are allowed to bring along their own food. Claygate has a surprisingly wide selection of takeaway food outlets just a few steps away on The Parade, a recent runner-up in the Great British High Street Awards. A reputedly excellent pizza van also rocks up on Tuesday and Saturday evenings. Team that with the reasonably priced drinks on offer (by Surrey standards, certainly) and you've got yourself a thrifty but fun night out.

Platform 3 is clearly already a popular community hub – the beating heart of what one might otherwise take to be a fairly somnolent place. Watching the glow of the lanterns in the crepuscular light, and hearing the cheery hubbub of habitués, it's difficult to believe that this is a little corner of a leafy commuter-belt town and not somewhere on the Continent, where one would feel rightly smug quaffing a local beer at such an establishment. It's very handy for the train home too.

Useful information

Open Feb–Dec, generally Thu and Fri 4–10.30pm, Sat 4–10pm, Sun 1–8.30pm, but these times are subject to change over the seasons. The pub is also open on 'bonus days', details of which are posted beforehand on the pub's Twitter account, the aptly named @SmallestPubInUK

Getting there by public transport

The most appropriate way to arrive, of course, is by train. Platform 3 is approximately a 5-second walk from the exit of Claygate railway station, which is on the New Guildford line between Guildford and London Waterloo.

Tiny Palace
Kew Palace, Surrey

It's fitting that Britain's smallest palace had comparatively humble beginnings. In fact, it had no connection with royalty at all, being built by that class of person thought rather beyond the pale by those in the ruling class, viz. a tradesman. Samuel Fortrey (the anglicised spelling of Forterie) had made such a vast fortune in silk by 1631 that he was able to have a fine mansion constructed on the Thames to the west of London. He had ordered another house on the site to be demolished, leaving only its undercroft, and raised his own house on top of it.

It wasn't until the following century that the mansion caught the eye of King George II and his wife Queen Caroline and the 'Dutch House' started its journey towards promotion to a royal palace. Caroline felt it would make a perfect residence for their three eldest daughters – Anne, Amelia and Caroline – and took a lease on it in 1728. This was followed by the accumulation of various other grand houses in the district, including the White House, which faced the

Dutch House and was rented by George and Caroline's son Prince Frederick. So began the love affair between Georgian monarchs and the residences at Kew, which was to endure for most of the 18th century.

The name of the Dutch House was coined in reference to Fortrey's supposed Dutch ancestry. Either there was some mix-up over this or the geography of the Low Countries was not a strong point of whoever came up with the label because Fortrey's forebears had come from Lille (which today is in northern France), which had actually been under the control of the Spanish Habsburgs when Fortrey's progenitors had lived there. In time, the silk merchant's mansion and other buildings nearby – including the White House – were collectively given the same status as the other many royal palaces in the hands of the British monarchy.

Go to Kew Gardens today and the Dutch House – virtually all that's left of the Kew Palace compound – is so unassuming that you could easily miss it. Almost hidden by trees on both sides, the four-storey residence has the look of a doll's house with its wide front aspect painted entirely in red and perfectly symmetrical set of white-framed windows. It was designed in the Artisan Mannerist style, which became popular for a while in the southeast of England. Its roof is punctured by three Dutch gables (which does at least tie the palace in some way to its misnomer)

and topped by an impressive array of tall chimneys.

Inside, the staff all come dressed in period costume to get you properly into a Georgian frame of mind. The rooms are festooned with paintings and decked out with chaises longues, the odd antique musical instrument and the sort of furniture that actually makes it look quite homely, which is a change from many a palace, albeit that everything is still rather on the formal side of swish. The poshest chamber is the Queen's Drawing Room, where a double marriage took place on 11 July 1818. Here, two of George III and Charlotte's sons, Princes William and Edward, married two German princesses, Adelaide of Saxe-Meiningen and Victoria of Saxe-Coburg-Saalfeld respectively. The wedding was conducted at Kew because Charlotte was too ill to leave the palace. She would die four months later in her bedroom. The future Queen Victoria was born to Edward and Victoria nine months after they married.

> The four-storey residence has the look of a doll's house, its wide front aspect painted entirely in red

It's also possible to visit the extensive royal kitchens, which were added to the palace by Frederick, Prince of Wales (George III's father). They not only give an insight into the vast undertaking it must have been to keep the royal court fed and watered but also offer a glimpse into the working conditions of those towards the other end of the social scale. The kitchens were locked up in 1818 on the death of Charlotte and remained undisturbed for nearly two centuries, leaving them preserved as if in aspic.

The most notorious period in the life of Kew Palace began towards the end of the 18th century. It was then that it became a very exclusive psychiatric hospital – its one and only patient being George III. The story of 'Mad' King George, as he is still known to this day, is an extremely sad one. Had he been a 21st-century king instead of a largely 18th-century one, we might have looked on his plight more sympathetically. He was on the throne for 60 years and for the first

28 of these he ruled in a manner that was no better or worse than many a monarch before him (though some might argue that the loss of Britain's American colonies during his reign was something of a faux pas). He was also a cultured individual with a keen interest in many areas of the arts and sciences. However, in 1788, when he was turning 50, George suffered an unidentified illness (probably not porphyria as is often cited) after which he was never the same again.

His rapid downward spiral into severe mental illness made him an embarrassment to the royal court and he was packed off to Kew Palace for treatment, or what passed for treatment in those days. It had been his favourite palace in earlier days and he and his family had taken to spending many summers in the various houses there, as well as using it as a weekend bolthole. Unfortunately, the return under these different circumstances was not a success. He was wont to spread his misery around his family, insisting that his younger daughters (he

It wasn't until 1898 that it was given a new lease of life by Queen Victoria, who had it opened to the public fathered 15 children, six of whom were girls) remain single and live with him at Kew, cut off from the greater part of society.

George was kept in the White House for four months during his first period of extreme mental affliction. The patient found himself there again in 1801, despite the fact that the building had been left to decay in the interim. His wife, Queen Charlotte, and various of her daughters occupied the Dutch House and whiled away their time hoping for the best. When the king was hauled back for a third time in 1804, the White House was no more – it had been torn down two years previously – and so he was kept in the service wing (later demolished) of the Dutch House and possibly in the Dutch House itself.

Eventually, the doctors who had attended him at Kew – treating him with leeches and emetics and forcing him to wear a straitjacket if he grew ungovernable – threw up their hands in despair at their inability to cure him. George was sent off to Windsor Castle which became his de facto prison thereafter. When he and Queen Charlotte died within two years of each other, Kew Palace fell out of favour and was more or less abandoned. It wasn't until 1898 that it was given a new lease of life by Queen Victoria, who had it opened to the public. Today it is managed by an independent charity called Historic Royal Palaces.

After you've seen the palace and dwelt upon the shortcomings of Georgian psychiatric care, you can visit the Great Pagoda, which was designed by Sir William Chambers for the royal family and completed in 1762.

It has recently undergone a major renovation to take it back to its 18th-century heyday.

Then you have the many other wonders of Kew Gardens to enjoy. These include the iconic Palm House, the Treetop Walkway and the Arboretum. Ironically, this last, with its 'living library' of 14,000 trees, is just the right place to provide balm for the soul and succour to the troubled mind.

Useful information

Royal Botanic Gardens, Kew, Richmond, Surrey TW9 3AE
Open daily end Mar–end Sep 10am–5.30pm (last admission 5pm)
Entry is via a ticket to Kew Gardens: adult: £11.50, children: (4–16) £2.50
U4s: free, concessions £10 | hrp.org.uk/kew-palace
NB Pagoda reopening in summer 2018

Getting there by public transport

London's Kew Gardens underground station, on the Richmond branch of the District line, is about 500yd from Kew Gardens' Victoria Gate. The London Overground from Stratford to Richmond also runs to Kew Gardens station.

Kew Bridge railway station can be reached from Waterloo and is about half a mile from the Elizabeth Gate. A 65 bus (tfl.gov.uk; 0343 222 1234) will take you from the station across the Thames to Lion Gate and Victoria Gate.

Alternatively, to add a little élan to your journey, in summer you can sail by riverboat up the Thames from Westminster Pier to Kew Pier or downstream from Hampton Court Pier (thamesriverboats.co.uk; 020 7930 2062)

13

Tiny Square
Pickering Place, London

In a city as populous and well known as London, it seems remarkable that the capital could possess an entire square that is practically secret. And yet that's the case with Pickering Place, not only the smallest square in London but one of the smallest in the land to boot.

As is only right, it takes a bit of finding. Tucked away in exclusive St James's, where the bygone era of gentlemen's clubs lives on, there's a very narrow covered alleyway that runs beside a venerable shop called Berry Bros. & Rudd.

Probably the oldest wine merchant in London, Berry Bros. has sold its vintage wares to the cognoscenti and the simply wealthy for more than three centuries. Their cellars burrow some way down Pall Mall and hold over 200,000 bottles of wine, making it the place to head for come the day of the Apocalypse.

The shop's history is inextricably bound up with that of Pickering Place. It was originally a grocer's and coffee-milling establishment founded by a woman popularly known as the Widow Bourne. Her son-in-law was James Pickering and it was he who built what became known as Pickering Court in 1731. Before that time there was what sounds like a rather scrubby little square known as Stroud's Court that was hemmed in by four 17th-century tenements. Pickering had these pulled down, replacing them with the buildings that stand there today.

Berry Bros. is also home to some very elderly and very large coffee scales. One day back in the 1760s – perhaps as a light-hearted jest or to settle a wager – they were used to weigh a customer. This kicked off a

Pickering Place is not only the smallest square in London but one of the smallest in the land

tradition that continues to this day (though by no means every customer is weighed, which will no doubt be a relief to most). So, if you want to know how many stones Lord Byron was packing when he visited, or how heavy the Aga Khan was, or the weight of any number of well-known figures from history, they're all recorded at Berry Bros. & Rudd. Hearteningly, the shop is still owned by members of the Berry and Rudd families, who are direct descendants of the Widow Bourne.

But the shop may well be a comparative youngster when contrasted with the narrow alleyway (one might almost say a tunnel) that runs down to the square. Some of the passageway's oak panelling is said to be Tudor and is reputedly the last surviving fragment of a real tennis court. It also had a brush with a much later date in history. Be sure to

look out for a small plaque near the entrance that states: 'In this building was the legation for the ministers from the Republic of Texas to the Court of St. James – 1842–1845 – Erected by the Anglo-Texan Society.'

This recalls the 10-year period when Texas (or rather Tejas) was a nation state. It broke away from Mexico in 1836 and was annexed by the US at the end of 1845, becoming a fully fledged state a couple of months later. The republic of Tejas was much larger than the US state of Texas is today and incorporated parts of four other modern states: Colorado, Kansas, Oklahoma and Wyoming. The diplomats representing the fledgling republic did their work in an office above Berry Bros. & Rudd. Like many diplomats before and since, they weren't always adept at paying their bills. They skipped the country leaving a debt of £160 in rent payable to their wine merchant landlords. It wasn't cleared until 1986 when a posse of Texans who could take the shame no more turned up at the shop with the overdue payment.

Passing into the paved square – really no more than a courtyard – two things are immediately noticeable, aside from just how small the square is. Firstly, it's a very irregular shape and, secondly, it's lit by gaslight

(the original lamps are still in situ). The Georgian edifices that crowd round the little open space take one immediately to another time and are, unsurprisingly, all listed buildings.

The tables and chairs of a French restaurant called Boulestin comprise most of the furniture in the square and contrive to make it appear even smaller than it already is. It's all but impossible to imagine that this cramped space was once a popular spot to fight duels. The privacy it afforded no doubt counted in its favour though. London dandy and cravat-inventor Beau Brummell is supposed to have fought one such encounter here and the square is purportedly the last place in England ever to have witnessed a duel (only Windsor claims a later date).

The courtyard's seclusion also made it a magnet for those intent on varying forms of vice and wickedness in the 18th century. Gambling dens flourished, it became a hotspot for bear-baiting (which was no doubt also the subject of frenzied wagers), and madams set up bawdy houses in the surrounding rooms.

Pickering Place had evidently cleaned up its act by the following century though because it was the home address for a while of the eminently respectable two-time Prime Minister Lord Palmerston – a man about as far removed from Beau Brummell as one is likely to get. A stone bust marks the premises in which he resided. The third man whose name is connected with the square is the author Graham Greene, who had a little flat here.

The days of authors casually renting a few rooms in the square are sadly over but there's no charge at all for anyone who merely fancies having a potter around the place. Probably best to leave the duelling pistols at home though.

Useful information

Off St James's Street, London SW1A 1EA

Always open (except when occasionally closed for private functions and filming) | Admission free

Getting there by public transport

Get yourself to London and then to Green Park Underground station, conveniently situated on the Piccadilly, Victoria and Jubilee lines. Come out onto Piccadilly, turn right and walk until you arrive at St James's Street. Turn right here and the entrance to Pickering Place is almost at the end, beside the Berry Bros. & Rudd wine shop, just before Pall Mall.

Tiny Park
Postman's Park, London

It has to be admitted, Postman's Park is actually one of the largest parks in the City of London. However, since the City has insisted on cramming itself with as much bone-achingly expensive office space as physics will allow, its parks are necessarily somewhat postage stamp-size affairs.

Postman's Park also has a unique feature among British parks: it is home to a space dedicated to those who have heroically given their lives to save others. Officially titled the Watts Memorial to Heroic Self-Sacrifice, it was established by the fine artist, sculptor and philanthropist George Frederic Watts in 1900 as a monument to those who make the ultimate gesture in altruism.

Postman's Park is a narrow strip of lawns, trees and flowerbeds wedged between St Bartholomew's Hospital in the west and the church of St Botolph's Without Aldersgate in the east. It's on land that was once occupied by three separate burial grounds: Christchurch, St Leonard's and St Botolph's.

Very popular as a lunch spot for local office workers, it gained its unusual name because it was once an equally popular lunch spot with postal workers based at the nearby General Post Office (which has long since disappeared).

The memorial that sets it apart from the thousands of lunchtime parks all over the nation is an understated one. Protected by an awning are glazed Doulton tiles, each one bearing a year, a name, sometimes an age and a few words about the heroic deed the individual carried out.

THOMAS·GRIFFIN
FITTERS·LABOURER
APRIL·12·1899 IN A
BOILER EXPLOSION AT A
BATTERSEA SUGAR REFINERY
WAS FATALLY SCALDED IN
RETURNING TO SEARCH
FOR HIS MATE

WALTER·PEART DRIVE
AND HARRY·DEAN FIREM.
OF THE WINDSOR EXPRES
ON JULY 18·1898
WHILST BEING SCALDED & BURN
SACRIFICED THEIR LIVES
SAVING THE TRAIN

JOSEPH ANDREW FORD
AGED 30·METROPOLITAN FIRE
BRIGADE· SAVED SIX PERSONS
FROM FIRE IN GRAY'S INN ROAD·
BUT IN HIS LAST HEROIC ACT
HE WAS SCORCHED TO DEATH
OCT·7·1871

AMELIA KENN
AGED 19·
DIED IN TRYING TO
SAVE HER SIS
FROM THEIR BVRNING
IN EDWARD'S LANE S
NEWINGTON OCT·

Watts was a radical socialist and an agitator for better working and living conditions for Britain's urban poor. In 1887 he floated an idea for a memorial to immortalise ordinary men and women who had given their lives for others. He believed it would be a good way of commemorating Queen Victoria's Golden Jubilee. However, the project didn't receive any backing. It was only 11 years later that Henry Gamble, vicar of St Botolph's Without Aldersgate, suggested to Watts that such a thing might be arranged in Postman's Park, some of which belonged to the church.

The memorial opened two years later. It comprised a 50ft awning that protected a wall with space for 120 tiles. At its unveiling just four tiles had been painted and installed. G F Watts died in 1904, leaving his widow, Mary, to continue the work.

One of the early tiles commemorates Elizabeth Boxall, a 17-year-old from Bethnal Green. In 1888, she 'died of injuries received in trying to save a child from a runaway horse'. Four people – Frederick Mills, A Rutter, Robert Durrant and F D Jones – met what were presumably terrible deaths 'in bravely striving to save a comrade at the sewage pumping works – East Ham – July 1st 1895'.

Although there are some instances of people attempting rescues from quicksand and following a boiler explosion at a sugar works, very often those who perished had saved others (or had attempted to save them) from fire or water, or from being hit by a train. Joseph Andrew Ford, for instance, saved six people from a burning building in 1871 'but in his last heroic act he was scorched to death'. Mary Rogers, stewardess on the passenger ferry *Stella*, 'self sacrificed by giving up her life belt and voluntarily going down in the sinking ship'. But most poignant are the stories of the many children, some as young as nine or ten, who saw someone in danger and did not hesitate to give up their own life to save them. Take a bow John Clinton, David Selves, Soloman Galaman, Harry Sisley, Herbert Maconoghu, Henry James Bristow and William Fisher.

The most recent tile celebrates the bravery of Leigh Pitt, a 30-year-old reprographic operator who leaped into a canal in Thamesmead, southeast London in June 2007, to

> It is home to a space dedicated to those who have heroically given their lives to save others

save the life of a nine-year-old boy. Although he was able to keep the boy above the surface of the water in a particularly deep part of the canal, there was no way of climbing up its high sides. Alerted by the shouts of Mr Pitt's fiancée, three other men jumped into the water to aid the rescue, but could not save Mr Pitt. He had been due to be married a few months later. The tablet was added in 2009, the first after a 78-year moratorium on new additions to the memorial.

The Watts memorial isn't the only noteworthy item in Postman's Park. There's a fountain and a sundial to be admired, and various exotic plants one wouldn't expect to flourish in central London. Look out for the most unusual pocket handkerchief tree (*Davidia involucrata*) whose large flowers do indeed resemble hankies, and the *Musa basjoo*, otherwise known as a Japanese banana (although it actually comes originally from southern China).

And if you can't get to the park in person, you can see it in the 2004 film *Closer*, which won two Golden Globes and a BAFTA. Based on the Patrick Marber play of the same name, it includes two scenes in Postman's Park. (There's a spoiler coming up here, so if you want to watch the film or the play without knowing this major plot twist, skip to the next page.) In the first, near the beginning of the film, characters played by Natalie Portman and Jude Law wander into the park by chance and come across the Watts Memorial to Heroic Self-Sacrifice. In the second, near the end, Jude Law is back in the park but this time on his own. He discovers that Natalie Portman's persona, Alice Ayres, is entirely invented. She has taken the name and backstory from the small fragment of biography on a tile in the memorial.

'Alice Ayres,' it reads, 'Daughter of a bricklayer's labourer who by intrepid conduct saved 3 children from a burning house in Union Street, Borough, at the cost of her own young life. April 24 1885.'

Useful information

St Martin's Le-Grand, London EC1A 4AS

Open all year round from 8am to 7pm or dusk, whichever is earlier.
Closed Christmas Day, Boxing Day and New Year's Day | Admission free

Getting there by public transport

St Paul's on the Central line is the nearest underground station.
It's a couple of minutes' walk from there along St Martin's Le-Grand, where you'll find an entrance on the left. Alternatively, Barbican station, on the Circle, Metropolitan and Hammersmith and City line, is only a little further away. Simply walk along Aldersgate Street, which becomes St Martin's Le-Grand, and the entrance is on the right. There's also an entrance to the park on King Edward Street.

Tiny Bridge
Poohsticks Bridge, East Sussex

Who doesn't love the work of A A Milne? There was the happy/sad poetry of 'When We Were Very Young' and 'Now We Are Six'. His three-dozen stage plays and half-dozen novels, every one of them forgotten. And, of course, the immortal *Winnie-the-Pooh* and *The House at Pooh Corner*, with their classic illustrations by E H Shepard, which have fired many a child's imagination (and possibly even taught them a lesson or two in life) since their publication in those far-off happy days of the Roaring Twenties, when all one had to worry about was mass unemployment, the return to the Gold Standard and the fact that penicillin hadn't been discovered yet.

All that hardly mattered though when one could enjoy Pooh's trap for Heffalumps, the Woozle that wasn't, and the almost unbearable pathos of Piglet tripping over on the way to see Eeyore, bursting the balloon that was supposed to be the eternally depressed donkey's birthday present. Perhaps most memorably of all, there was the story regarding the invention of the game of Poohsticks.

Winnie-the-Pooh, tripping over (there's quite a lot of tripping over in the Pooh stories) by a bridge, involuntarily drops a fir cone into a stream (or 'river' as he prefers to call it). Initially irritated by this, he notes with wonder a few moments later that the fir cone is now floating on the other side of the bridge, not the side over which he spilled it. This gives him an idea. He stands on the bridge and drops two fir cones into the water to see which of them will be quicker at getting to the other side. He repeats the game, each time trying to predict which fir cone will win. He ends up guessing right 36 times out of 64 (a 56.25% success rate), which is not bad for a supposed Bear With Very Little Brain. He adapts the game into a straight race involving two or more players, but using sticks instead of fir cones (the former being simpler to mark). Had he found some way of copyrighting the event, he'd be a rich bear now, instead of spending his days under glass with his friends at the New York Public Library.

The footbridge that inspired A A Milne to include this episode was in Posingford Wood, crossing a stream heading for the River Medway. Milne lived close by with his wife and son (Christopher Robin) at Cotchford Farm. This placed him on the doorstep of the Ashdown Forest and just a little to the southwest of Hartfield, a village renowned for its once glorious football team and the Pooh Corner shop, dedicated to all things Poohian.

For a short and otherwise obscure footbridge, an awful lot is known about its history. It was constructed in 1907 by a team of 14 led by one John Charles Osman. (See? We even know the builder's middle name.) It was clearly very skilfully crafted because it survived well into the 1970s when a major restoration took place. The revamped bridge was opened by Christopher Robin Milne in 1979. This lasted rather less time and was replaced at the turn of the century by the current wooden bridge which, happily, is still very much in the style of the original with its fenced sides on whose bottom rail Pooh could just about get his chin.

The stream is still the same lazy 'river', and indulging in a little Poohsticks where Pooh, Rabbit and Piglet could often be found playing the game – or simply 'doing Nothing' – is a simple but profound joy.

The Ashdown Forest is actually a mixture of heathland and woodland. A vast 6,500-acre swathe of Wealden Sussex, it has seen life as a Roman estate, a mustering point for soldiers ready to repel Napoleon's hordes

> The revamped bridge was opened by Christopher Robin Milne in 1979

(the marks of the camp kitchens are still visible), and a royal hunting ground. But the most deeply satisfying thing about the forest is that it really doesn't take all that much to imagine Winnie-the-Pooh and his friends wandering around in it. The 100 Aker Wood (actually named the Five Hundred Acre Wood) is an easy walk from Poohsticks Bridge and further exploration will unveil Eeyore's gloomy place (at Wren's Warren Valley – be sure to visit on a dank and dreary day), Roo's Sandy Pit and the North Pole (site of).

When you go, do take along a copy of *The House at Pooh Corner* to read on the bridge – the incident in which Eeyore finds himself floating down the river while the others are playing Poohsticks is still laugh-out-loud funny even after all these years.

Useful information

Ashdown Forest, East Sussex

Open all the time | Admission free | ashdownforest.org | 01342 823583.
Be sure to bring your own sticks because there'll be a paucity of them near the bridge, for obvious reasons. A handy map showing the bridge (and other Pooh-related locations) can be found at just-pooh.com

Getting there by public transport

Head for East Grinstead railway station, the terminus of a line that runs through East Croydon from central London. From outside the station take the 291 bus (metrobus.co.uk; 01293 449191) to Cat Street in Upper Hartfield. Turn right off Cat Street into the narrow Cotchford Lane following the bridleway sign. After just over half a mile, at the point where Cotchford Lane turns sharp left, turn right along another bridleway for a few hundred yards to arrive at Poohsticks Bridge.

16

Tiny Town
Fordwich, Kent

With just 381 inhabitants, a figure that doesn't even mark it out as a village of any great size, the little community of Fordwich on the Great Stour has somehow contrived to be the smallest town in Britain. Although this is disputed by the folk of Watlington (see page 59), it is an inescapable fact that Fordwich is not only smaller in terms of its physical size but has a population that is less than a seventh of the Oxfordshire metropolis.

The only contentious detail is whether it should really be classed as a town at all. In antiquity, it certainly held that status. Although we first hear mention of it in AD 675 as the tiny Saxon settlement of Fordewicum ('place by a ford'), it began to grow as boats forged up the Stour from the English Channel and, coming to Fordwich, the highest navigable point on the river, used it as a port. In the Middle Ages, the mouth of the Stour was just 4 or 5 miles away, and the river was very broad – indeed, it was more or less a long inlet of the sea. It flowed into the Wantsum Channel, which in those days cut the Isle of Thanet off from the mainland, making it into a proper island – unlike today. Canterbury cathedral was rebuilt of stone from Caen in France which came that very way: it was unloaded at Fordwich to be transported the 2 miles to where the masons were waiting with chisels in hand.

Henry II granted Fordwich a Merchant Guild Charter in 1184, turning the thriving village into a town at the stroke of a royal quill, or, more likely, the press of a royal

seal. By the 13th century the freshly minted town had a formal association with the Cinque Ports (the original five being Hastings, Romney, Hythe, Dover and Sandwich). These had been granted a great deal of autonomy by Edward the Confessor in return for equipping him with a 57-ship navy to patrol the Channel, a custom that the Norman kings continued. The difficulties of producing the ships and crews by themselves eventually led the officialdom at the Cinque Ports to call on three other towns to help out. These were called 'limbs' and Fordwich, which already had ties to Sandwich, was one of them. As a supplier of ships and crew to the king's navy, the importance of the little town on the Stour was assured.

One glance at a map today, however, is enough to show just how small and seemingly inconsequential Fordwich is. Lurking just outside Canterbury, like a pea on a football, it's even dwarfed by its close neighbour Sturry, a town that no one outside of Sturry has actually ever heard of. Fordwich's demise came about for two reasons. The silting up of the Wantsum Channel by the late 1700s pushed the mouth of the Stour towards Sandwich, forcing shipping to take a much longer and more circuitous journey along a much narrower waterway. Furthermore, as the power of the Cinque Ports dwindled, so did that of its limbs. In 1830 the port at Fordwich finally closed, and precisely 50 years later the community had its status as a town stripped from it.

And that might have been that had it not been for a local government overhaul in 1972 in which Fordwich was made a town again, a decision seemingly based on little more than nostalgia for its former glories. The council meets in the Old Town Hall, which was built during the reign of Henry VIII. It calls itself a town council and whoever is the chair is also the mayor. In strictly legal terms, however, the community it serves is a civil parish, which is at the root of Watlington's counterclaim to the smallest town title.

While we're on the subject, it's probably a good time to point out that there are more runners and riders competing for that honour than one might imagine. There's Manningtree in Essex, which coincidentally also lies on the River Stour, albeit a different one. The town's population of around 700 is squeezed into just 50 acres (at high tide). Cumbria's Broughton-in-Furness is even more sparsely populated, running to just over 500 inhabitants, while Llanwrtyd Wells (see page 187) in Powys has 850. No doubt they all have very compelling arguments but life is really very brief.

More pressing is whether the nation's most likely smallest town actually has anything of worth to offer the visitor to its shores. The port is long gone, of course, but the river still flows through here, looking particularly bucolic as it passes through fields and under a bridge. To the east of Fordwich, on either side of the waterway, there are also lakes and marshes – fragmentary remains of the inlet that brought the town into existence.

There are plenty of pleasingly old buildings that have survived to tell of the town's heyday too. The church of St Mary the Virgin may no longer host regular services but it's still open daily. With parts of it over 900 years old, it's the most venerable building in Fordwich and sports a fine spire.

It's also a living record of a flood that occurred in the 15th century. The waters from the nearby Stour have caused the walls of the church to lean, though thankfully not so much that it's in any imminent danger of collapse. The paintings, fixtures and fittings mostly date from the 17th century (though the font is from the 12th) but the one really curious item

Lurking just outside Canterbury, like a pea on a football, it's even dwarfed by its close neighbour Sturry

is much older. It's a carved stone a little over 5ft long that is believed to have been a reliquary installed in the church to contain some body part (or parts) of a saint. Since it probably dates from around 1100, it's suggested that it might once have held some or all of St Augustine of Canterbury.

The church plays a role in the 1944 Powell and Pressburger film *A Canterbury Tale*, starring Sheila Sim and Eric Portman. Filmed in and around Fordwich, it provides an excellent guide to how the town looked in the last war as its characters (excessively loosely) play out a propaganda-heavy version of Chaucer's masterpiece *The Canterbury Tales*.

Unusually, St Mary the Virgin is also available to hire for exclusive use overnight. This is one of the places of worship looked after by the Churches Conservation Trust in which it's possible to engage in a bit of champing (i.e. 'church camping' – their word, not mine, and they've trademarked it too). Camp beds, lanterns, a loo and a few other accoutrements are laid on for guests who then have the unfamiliar experience of sleeping the night in a church, possibly near the former resting place of some sections of a saint.

There's an attractive 16th-century house in the High Street that started life as a pair of cottages, and another Grade II listed building of the same period called Watergate House which became a soap factory for a while around 1800. But the *pièce de résistance* is the Old Town Hall on King Street. Constructed in 1544, it is perhaps not only the oldest town hall still serving the purpose for which it was built but the smallest one too. And possibly the only one to display a genuine ducking stool.

Rather remarkably, it still has its original timbers inside as well as the fetching herringbone-style exterior brickwork its Tudor craftsmen constructed. For a period there was a jail on the ground floor. In 1855, the last three men to find themselves incarcerated there were charged with poaching Fordwich trout. This singularly large fish had been made famous in Izaak Walton's bestselling book *The Compleat Angler*, published two centuries earlier, in 1653, when the Commonwealth was just getting going and hope was still in the air.

Upstairs was the courtroom, where the cases of those held below were heard. Those accused of crimes put their side of the story at what is known as 'the pleading bar'. To the rear of the building, the Crane House holds a crane used for offloading goods – mostly bound for Canterbury – from boats that made the journey up the Stour. Of course, none of these functions have much to do with what we think of as the business of a town hall, but in the Middle Ages fine buildings such as this were expensive to produce and so often found themselves serving many diverse functions as a way of getting every farthing's worth of value out of them.

For a place so small it's a surprise to find that there's a choice of pubs to repair to after all the excitement of perusing time-worn buildings. Naturally enough, they too are rather old. The George and Dragon dates its origins back to the 15th century and stood in as the 'Hand of Glory' in *A Canterbury Tale*. The Fordwich Arms, meanwhile, is a wonderful brick confection with huge chimneys, an open fire and an oak-panelled dining room. From the beer garden there's an excellent view of the church spire.

And if you should ever wish to leave – and don't happen to have a rowing boat to hand in order to drift away along the Great Stour – the most stylish way to do so would be to head out on the Stour Valley Walk. The long-distance footpath follows the river for 51 miles from its source at Lenham to its meeting with the sea at Pegwell Bay. No longer does the Stour create tiny towns but it still cuts a swathe through a most charming corner of the Garden of England.

Useful information

Old Town Hall: Open 1.30pm–4pm Easter Sat–Mon, May and Aug bank holidays, Sun from May to Sep, Wed in Aug | Adult £2, children U14 free fordwichtown.org

Church of St Mary the Virgin: Churches Conservation Trust | Open daily 10am–3pm | Admission free | To stay overnight visit champing.co.uk

Getting there by public transport

Take the train to Sturry railway station on the Ashford to Ramsgate line. The centre of Fordwich is a 10-minute walk away along Sturry Hill and then Fordwich Road.

Tiny Theatre
Tom Thumb Theatre, Kent

The coastal town of Margate has had something of a roller-coaster existence. This turns out to be rather apt since its well-known (and recently resurrected) pleasure park Dreamland Margate is the home of Britain's oldest roller coaster.

The town's other claims to fame stem from its associations with two artists – J M W Turner and Tracey Emin (who characterised her home town as 'romantic, sexy and weird', a description one can't imagine coming from the mouth of the creator of *The Fighting Temeraire*) – its subterranean Shell Grotto and for being namechecked in a hit single by Chas & Dave. Once a byword for popular seaside resorts that had slid into embarrassing decline, the town is now very much on the rise again.

Margate is the home of the recently opened Turner Contemporary Gallery, retro shops and trendy cafés. Its reputation as the ringleader of the country's latest crop of thrusting young Turks was cemented in 2015 when it had the dubious honour of having the UK's fastest-rising house prices (a giddying 24.2%) anywhere outside London.

And yet for all this, Margate's importance in the history of the dramatic arts in Britain remains woefully overlooked. Not only is the resort the home of the second-oldest working theatre in the UK (take a bow, Theatre Royal), it also possesses Britain's smallest Victorian theatre, or at least Britain's smallest theatre in a Victorian building. The Tom Thumb is truly one of a kind. Sitting in a glorious location a little back from the sea on the town's esplanade, it's so very eclectic and so very glamorous

that it would be worth going to visit even if the owners never put another show on again (though happily there's little sign of that happening).

The Tom Thumb was not really meant to be a theatre at all. It was built in 1896 as a coach house – the equivalent of a garage for a carriage and with a necessarily higher ceiling. The ground floor of the building, with its red wooden panels and little windows, actually gives it more the look of a former fire station. But that's by no means the oddest thing about the building's appearance. It has a very unusually ornate balcony that wraps around the front and one side that is a blend of Japanese and Swiss Alpine architectural styles. Perhaps understandably, that's not a mix that has ever caught on.

Carriages gave way to cars in the years following the building's erection and, inevitably, the coach house became a large garage. By the 1980s, however, it had become very

It's so very eclectic and so very glamorous that it would be worth going to visit even if the owners never put another show on again

dilapidated and could have been lost to the nation. Thankfully, mother and daughter Lesley and Sarah Parr-Byrne saw the construction's possibilities. They bought it in 1984, completely restored it and converted it for use as a theatre. Not a partnership to do things by halves, the Parr-Byrnes chose to give it the authentic look of a Victorian playhouse. Step inside and all thoughts of Japan and the Alps are left behind. This is a red-hued slice of 19th-century Britain: from the flocked wallpaper and the stage curtain hanging in luxurious folds to the 51 velvet seats in seven neat rows. Go upstairs and you'll find a shabby-chic cocktail bar in which the eponymous drinks are served in jam jars (which is perhaps not quite the Victorian way).

But back in the auditorium, when the curtains are drawn aside they reveal a strikingly compact space beyond. At just 10ft by 7ft it's apparently the smallest stage in a British theatre. It means you're unlikely ever to see a production of

Les Miserables here (although the two-man National Theatre of Brent could probably give it a go).

However, there is a surprising variety in the acts that do tread these rather minimal boards. A packed season will often include elements such as experimental drama, performance art, spoken-word nights, storytelling, DJs, solo musicians, live bands and burlesque, while every year the Tom Thumb's pantomime is a sell-out.

Despite its size, the venue attracts well-known actors such as Rita Tushingham and Pauline McLynn and theatre companies such as Shunt. Perhaps, some day, Margate will be best known for being the place with the brilliant tiny theatre. Until then, the Tom Thumb remains a cracking venue for a night out.

Useful information

2 Eastern Esplanade, Cliftonville, Margate CT9 2LB
See website for performance times and tickets | tomthumbtheatre.co.uk
01843 221791

Getting there by public transport

Travel to Margate railway station, which is on the line to the Kent coast from London that carries on to Ramsgate and points beyond. From the station the theatre is a pleasant 1½-mile walk along the Thanet Coastal Path. Alternatively, walk the very short distance to Canterbury Road near the junction with Albert Road and take the number 33 bus (stagecoachbus.com; 03456 002299) to the north end of Sweyn Road, from where it's a brief stroll along Eastern Esplanade to the theatre.

Tiny Church
St Ives Bridge Chapel, Cambridgeshire

Should you visit St Ives in Cambridgeshire and make it down to the southern end of the agreeable market town, you might be forgiven for thinking you had been suddenly whisked away to France. Spanning the River Great Ouse is a quite magnificent 15th-century stone bridge that wouldn't look at all out of place if it were casually vaulting the Loire or the Lot.

What makes the bridge at St Ives all the more special is a curious box-like structure about halfway across that appears to be dangling off a parapet. On closer inspection, the church-like gothic windows might give the game away. The box is a chapel. Although it might be fairer to say that the box was once a chapel because in its long life it has been many things and the last time it was actually a chapel was back in the 16th century.

A bridge may sound like a curious place to put a chapel but there was a period in English history – from the late medieval era up to the Reformation – when it was all the

rage. The idea behind them was that travellers could receive a blessing from a monk there and perhaps some spiritual encouragement. Travelling was a dangerous and uncertain business back in the Middle Ages and those on the move would doubtless have been gratified to come across a sanctuary where they might pray for deliverance from the many evils that might await them on the road, even if they had to pay a small toll at the same time for crossing the bridge.

The practice of building chapels or chantries on river crossings was also common on the Continent, but the Reformation in the 16th century did for most of Britain's bridge chapels, which were either destroyed or put to use for some other purpose. The St Ives chapel escaped demolition but never regained its status as a holy place. It's just one of four British survivors, joining those at Wakefield, Rotherham and Bradford-upon-Avon. Wakefield's spent some time as a cheese shop; for over 20 years Rotherham's was a tobacconist; while Bradford-upon-Avon's chapel became the town's lock-up. It seems that the destiny of every bridge chapel was to be ill-used. However, these fates were as nothing when compared with that of the chapel at St Ives.

The monks of Ramsey Abbey threw the first bridge across the Great Ouse at St Ives in 1107. It was made of wood but lasted three centuries until replaced in 1425 by the current stone structure. The chapel was added one year later on top of a pier widened for the purpose. It was dedicated to St Leger, a Burgundian bishop who had his eyes drilled and

his tongue cut out on his way to sainthood.

However, the building would serve as a chapel for little more than a century. The rolling tide of the Reformation, which swept away so much of Catholicism and its way of doing things, engulfed the chapel in 1539. Initially, it was converted into a residence for the local prior. In later years it saw service as a doctor's surgery, a toll-keeper's house and, most inappropriately of all, a pub called Little Hell. As might be deduced from such a name, it was not an inn with a reputation for decorum and moderation. The landlord is also reputed to have kept pigs in the crypt, which by that time (the mid-19th century) had long since been converted into a cellar.

The former chapel gained a couple of storeys in 1736, though the additions – stone utilitarian boxes more reminiscent of 1960s brutalism – were not a success. Photographs of the unfortunate structure taken in the early part of the 20th century

A bridge may seem like a curious place to put a chapel but there was a period in English history when it was all the rage

show it towering awkwardly over the bridge as if the two had been fused together by a model-maker who had forgotten to ensure they were both the same scale. It was finally agreed to remove the offending storeys in 1930 – though the decision was not taken on aesthetic grounds but because the extra weight was damaging the foundations.

In the meantime, the bridge had been going through some rather drastic changes itself. Oliver Cromwell (who lived in St Ives for five years) had two arches at the southern end ripped out in 1643 and replaced with a drawbridge so that he could use the Great Ouse as a barrier to Cavalier forces making their way to London from Lincolnshire. Happily, 70 years later the drawbridge was replaced. However, if you look closely at the southern end of the bridge, you'll notice that although the stonework matches the original crossing very well, those two arches are rounded while all the rest are gothic.

There's a simplicity to the interior of the chapel. One imagines that during the time it functioned as a source of spiritual nourishment for those on the move it would have been adorned with statuary and an altar of some sort. Nowadays, aside from its gothic windows, there's not a great deal to suggest that it was once a house of God. However, a steep and narrow flight of winding stairs leads down to the crypt, which has more the character of a church with its whitewashed walls, stone floor and oak-beamed ceiling.

When you descend the staircase you are walking in the footsteps of Sir Harry Secombe, a man not known for his svelte physique, who somehow managed to squeeze himself down them during the filming of an episode of *Songs of Praise*. A door from the crypt opens out onto a Juliet balcony. Step out and you find yourself in the unusual position of not only being right on top of the river but in mid-stream too.

The same year that the building was relieved of its burdensome extra levels, it was restored to more or less the condition it was in when first built, albeit that a new roof had to be constructed for it. Further restoration was undertaken in 2000 and the chapel (along with the bridge itself) is now a scheduled ancient monument.

Nowadays, cars are banned from the bridge (another crossing was built downstream in 1980) and only certain goods vehicles may use it. When they are absent, the bridge is returned to a level of tranquillity not known since the days when one travelled either on foot or on horseback.

Although it is not used for its original purpose, we may assume that the chapel has found some sort of peace at last.

Modern-day travellers, meanwhile, are left to seek their blessings in railway buffet bars and motorway service stations, both places where those sorts of pickings tend to be very slim indeed.

Useful information

Usually open at weekends in the summer, but staffed by volunteers so times and days of opening may not be consistent. However, to gain access you can either book an appointment in advance via the Norris Museum (norrismuseum.org.uk; 01480 497314) or call there at The Broadway, St Ives PE27 5BX (open May–Sep Mon–Sat 10am– 4pm, Sun 1–4pm, Oct–Apr Mon–Sat 10am–4pm) to pick up the chapel key (£20 deposit required) Admission free | Donation to the museum appreciated

Getting there by public transport

It's as easy as pie to get to St Ives – simply take a train to Huntingdon railway station on the line from London King's Cross to Peterborough. From there the very frequent 'The Busway' B bus (stagecoachbus.com; 01480 453159) will hurtle you to St Ives in under half an hour. From St Ives bus station walk west along Market Hill and turn left when you reach Bridge Street, which will take you to the chapel.

Tiny Pub
The Nutshell, Suffolk

'A mummified cat hangs from the ceiling of a bar' does sound rather like the start of a joke, though not necessarily a very entertaining one. However, in the case of The Nutshell, a pub nestled on a pedestrianised street in the historic market town of Bury St Edmunds, it's simply a statement of fact. The blackened feline husk has been staring blindly down on customers ever since it was discovered during construction work.

Despite the emergence of the even titchier Platform 3 in Claygate (see page 63), The Nutshell still claims to be Britain's smallest pub (and, to be fair, the customers of the former do sit outside to drink). Indeed, the Suffolk tavern still has the backing of Guinness World Records, which, if it can't get a record about a pub right, should really think about changing its sponsors. The Nutshell's interior measures just 15ft by 7ft, or much less than half the size of a typical shipping container. The bar runs the length of the pub, with the customers propping it up or sitting on benches in the large windows that make up the two sides of the pub that face the street. Punters can either sup on the usual suspects such as Carling lager or Strongbow cider, or perhaps try one or two Suffolk ales, which are always on tap.

Curiously, for a space so small The Nutshell is filled with an awful lot of odds and ends that are not strictly prerequisites to the smooth running of a pub. The cat is certainly not in want of company. Hanging off the ceiling, the walls or anywhere else

where room can be found, there are the severed heads of animals, various hats, keys, old framed photos, militaria, awards, the large wooden propeller of an aeroplane (because why not?) and much else besides. Meanwhile, the ceiling and upper parts of the walls are plastered with hundreds of banknotes from overseas.

The Nutshell has been going a lot longer than many a tiny pub. It opened in 1867, the same year that Madame Curie was born and the first ship passed through the Suez Canal. The building itself is somewhat older and for many years the premises were dedicated to the sale of fruit. Indeed, it was a local fruiterer called John Stebbing who took over the pub in 1873. It was the Stebbings who put their mark on the place and shaped what it is today. The appurtenances that adorn the ceiling and walls reflect to some degree the lives of the various members of the family. Had you been able to drop by in the early days of the establishment, you'd have stumbled into what the Stebbings called a Museum of Art and Curiosities. It sounds like quite the place. According to the current owners' potted history of the pub, 'They offered visitors a wide variety of attractions including ancient musical instruments, relics from past wars and works of art in ivory and cardboard.' On display there were also cork models of prominent buildings in the town and of famous London landmarks such as Nelson's Column and Windsor Castle.

The year after the arrival of the Stebbings, the building was sold to an F W King of King's Brewery. The company would merge a decade or so later with another Bury St Edmunds brewer in the hands of the Greene family. This proved to be a significant step on the way to becoming a mighty empire. Greene King, as the new company was called, has grown to become the largest public house owner and brewer in Britain today.

The pub has connections with another giant, though from a very different walk of life. It means that fans of the late lamented John Peel may care to pay homage here. The disc jockey, who made his home in Suffolk, turned up at the pub in 1984 to greet various dimmer lights in the Radio 1 firmament who were treating the good people of Bury St Edmunds to a roadshow. Broadcast to a spellbound nation was a successful attempt to get the greatest number of customers into the bar. The final total of 102 (and a dog) beat the previous record by one (though only equalled the number of dogs). It's not clear whether the great man was one of the 102 involved in the feat but he was photographed standing outside in a frankly snazzy bomber jacket, clasping a pint and looking cheery, so one assumes probably not.

Those who enjoy picking out a famous face in a photo from days gone by should take a look at the pub's scrapbook, which includes various celebrities who have had a drink here. The comedian Al Murray, aka 'The Pub Landlord', went so far as to send a photo of himself to adorn the wall to commemorate The Nutshell's stint as his 'Pub of the Week'. After your visit, you can also stake your place among the immortals by adding a message and perhaps even uploading a photograph to the pub's online guestbook. Your future biographers will surely bless you for it.

Useful information

17 The Traverse, Bury St Edmunds, Suffolk IP33 1BJ
Open daily 11am–11pm | thenutshellpub.co.uk | 01284 764867

Getting there by public transport

Bury St Edmunds railway station can be found on the line between Stowmarket in Suffolk and Ely in Cambridgeshire. The Nutshell is half a mile due south through the town to The Traverse, a pedestrianised area between Skinner Street and Cornhill.

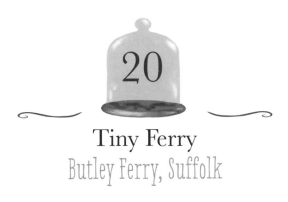

Tiny Ferry
Butley Ferry, Suffolk

The Butley River is not one that hits the headlines all that often. Rising up in the hidden depths of Rendlesham Forest, it makes its way so unobtrusively eastwards through a morass of cuts, ponds and streams that you'd be very hard pressed indeed to follow it with a map in hand, for cartographers themselves seem to have little idea of its route.

Only when it decides to turn abruptly south at a hamlet called Butley Mills does it get going in earnest. Even then it is little more than a stream with pretensions and is referred to as Butley Creek.

It spends its entire life in obscurity. Its brush with the tiny cluster of houses and art studio at Butley Mills is as gregarious as it ever becomes. It passes mostly unseen for the rest of its short run down to the River Ore, whence its waters slide along Orford Beach for miles before slipping into the sea, as if they were a nervous diver standing for an age on the edge of a pool before timidly sliding in at last.

About 3 miles downstream of Butley Mills, in a quilt of open fields, at a point some way from the nearest road, and just before the arrival of a worm-like tributary called The Tang, Butley Creek describes a little dogleg. And here there is a ferry crossing. It is in such an apparently inconsequential spot that one could forgive approaching walkers and cyclists – seeing the arcing blue line of the Butley River on a map and not a bridge spanning it for miles – for abandoning even the least scintilla of hope that they might cross the waterway without some not insignificant dampening of their person. But it is just at this spot that the good volunteers of the Alde and Ore Association turn up at weekends and bank holidays from spring to autumn. They row all-comers safely over 70yd of briskly flowing waters. Those heading east are spared the extra 4 miles they would have to travel to reach the picturesque village of Orford and its castle. Those heading west avail themselves of a similar shortcut as they make their way along the coast to distant Bawdsey and the ferry across the Deben to Felixstowe. The crossing is an integral part of the Regional Cycle Route 41 from Felixstowe to Bramfield and also offers walkers a chance to hop on or off the Suffolk Coast Path. With the boat being so little – it affords just about enough room for two passengers and their bicycles – it's reputed to be the smallest licensed rowed ferry in Europe.

The first customers here were probably conveyed across the Butley River (the name is always that way about) as long ago as the 16th century and perhaps considerably before that. In those days, when none but the wealthy owned a means of conveyance, the chance to save oneself a long trek on the way to or from the market at Orford, especially when laden down with goods, must have made it worth the farthing or whatever was the nominal fare charged by the early ferrymen. The service ran for at least six days a week, apparently without interruption, until 1920. It might all have ended there, but the ferry crossing was rescued from the oxbow lake of history by one man: Bryan Rogers. Having had a successful business career, he retired early to Suffolk and took it upon himself to resuscitate the service. He heroically embarked upon three years of manual labour, shifting 50 tonnes of gravel and muck from the badly silted-up river, and building jetties on both banks. He bought a rowing boat and in 1994 the Butley River ferry was operational once more. The following year, his first full season, he

> With just enough room for two passengers and their bicycles, it's the smallest licensed rowed ferry in Europe

had over 200 customers and reckoned that after paying insurance and the licence fee he had made a loss of about £300, not that that worried him unduly.

'I reckon this has been a ferry site for 600 years,' he told *The Independent* in 1995. 'I believe running the ferry is a worthwhile contribution to the local community. People say it is a ferry to nowhere but it is used by coastal walkers and birdwatchers.'

Nowadays there's a whole team of selfless volunteers at the oars to carry on Mr Rogers' work. They don the traditional broad-brimmed hats worn by Suffolk farmworkers and ferrymen since time immemorial. Each year they transport across the creek more than a thousand passengers and about 500 bicycles. The money they raise by their toil goes to a fund that helps keep the river defences in good repair. Understandably, working with such a diminutive craft at a point where the river is still tidal, the volunteers don't operate if the wind gets up to force 5 or beyond, so it's always a good idea to have a quick glance at a weather forecast before setting off in hope of a passage.

Lovers of fluvial voyages will no doubt be sad to learn that efforts made in 2011 to revive the ferry route between Orford and Aldeburgh fizzled out. Still, at least it's possible to cycle or walk to Walberswick, thence to be rowed once more – this time across the Blyth – and on to Aldeburgh (see page 112).

Useful information

Near Capel St Andrew
Sailings from Easter Sat to last Sun in Oct at weekends and bank holidays only | 11am–4pm, weather permitting | Adult and older children £2, children U11 £1.50, bicycles £1.50 (no tandems)
aldeandore.org | 07913 672499
To become a volunteer rower of the ferry, contact Tim Dudgeon on 01728 648493

Getting there by public transport

The closest railway is Melton, on the Ipswich to Lowestoft line, about 7 miles northwest. It's possible to take the 71 bus (PF Travel; 01394 388333) to Capel St Andrew, from where it's just over a mile to the ferry.

21

Tiny Pier
Southwold Pier, Suffolk

Roll up! Roll up! Come see the incredible shrinking pier! When the finest pier on the Suffolk Coast started life in 1900 it stretched 810ft into the southernmost reaches of the North Sea.

In 1934, the landing stage at the end was lost in a storm. When World War II brought with it the threat of a German invasion, the pier suffered the indignity of having a section chopped out of it to prevent it from being used by the Axis forces. Worse still, in 1941 a loose mine collided with it, blowing a rather less methodical hole in the structure. Come 1955, another fierce storm struck the coast and took the far half of the pier clean away with it. Just when it looked like things couldn't get worse, 1979 saw yet another storm blow in and the pier was reduced to a stub just 60ft long, which made the tiddly pier at Burnham-on-Sea (see page 39) look positively gargantuan by comparison.

It was only when Southwold's disappearing pier was purchased in 1987 by one Chris Iredale that the process began to be reversed. It took a lot of perseverance but by 2002 the pier had gained the length it has today: 623ft. To put that into perspective, the Palace Pier at Brighton is nearly three times as long, Southport Pier is six times longer and Britain's longest pier at Southend stretches over 10 times further into the briny.

Visiting it today, you wouldn't really guess that Southwold Pier had had such a turbulent and traumatic history. It looks every inch a charming and rather jolly affair: a slender and elegant jetty on which bright white hut-like buildings with grey roofs have been squeezed into position. The structure as a whole fits in very well with Southwold's opinion of itself as a rather stylish if slightly genteel place. The view of the pier from the streets of brightly coloured beach huts that line the promenade has certainly struck a chord with photographers.

The pier's original function was to enable holidaymakers on steamships up from London to disembark at the resort. To facilitate this it had a landing stage at the far end (from above, the pier would have looked like a 'T'). As a nod to the earlier incarnation, the pier today has a similar construction, although this time it's devoted to the noble cause of giving visitors more room to wander about.

But it's the pier's various attractions that really set it apart, particularly the Under the Pier Show (which, despite its name, is actually on the pier). This comprises a brilliantly eccentric compilation of coin-operated machines conceived and built by the inventor Tim Hunkin. Among other pursuits you can take out your frustrations regarding the ongoing fall-out from the 2008 financial crash by playing 'Whack a Banker' (or engage in an act of self-flagellation if you are one); cause or avert a nuclear disaster according to your level of dexterity handling plutonium rods; or if you're feeling in a compassionate state of mind, help a granny and her Zimmer frame across the road.

Elsewhere, there's a Quantum Tunnelling Telescope – something one hopes that every pier might have in the future. For the time being, this is the only one. Another of Tim Hunkin's creations, it resembles a sort of low-fi sci-fi version of an ordinary pay-per-view telescope as seen on seafronts the country over. Look through it though and you don't get a blurry image of the horizon. Instead, it enables you to see everything there is to see in the North Sea all at once (including mermaids). You'll never look at the space–time continuum in the same way ever again. Meanwhile, a startlingly good steam-punk water clock puts on a show every half hour.

Traditionalists will be pleased to learn there's also a wall of mirrors and a pavilion dedicated to conventional slot-machine games. Refreshments are provided by the Beach Café while the Treat Parlour caters for the sweet of tooth. A gift shop called the Treasure Chest will relieve you of any spare cash you may have left after that.

Mr Iredale's efforts won Britain's Pier of the Year Award in 2002. It's changed hands a couple of times

since then but seems to be going from strength to strength, which is certainly not true of all Britain's piers. Apparently there are plans to build a hotel on it as well, which sounds ambitious since there's not a great deal of room to spare.

After you've enjoyed the delights of the pier, you can take a very pleasant stroll along the front past those ranks of brightly coloured beach huts and on to the tiny Walberswick Ferry. There you can be rowed over the River Blyth, a service that has operated since 1236. The chances are you'll soon be coming back the other way in search of one last game of 'Whack a Banker'.

Useful information

North Parade, Southwold IP18 6BN

Open daily from 9am, closing times change according to the seasons.

The Beach Café opens from 9am but attractions on the pier generally open at 10am | Admission free

southwoldpier.co.uk | 01502 722105

Tim Hunkin: The brilliant inventor's website (timhunkin.com) gives some insights into his highly original machines

Walberswick Ferry, River Blyth | Sailings daily from Jun to Sep as well as weekends in Apr–May 10am–5pm, weather and tide permitting (closed for lunch weekdays 12.30–2pm) | One-way £1 per person, children U5 free, £1 per bicycle (no tandems) | walberswickferry.com

Getting there by public transport

From Halesworth railway station, on the Ipswich to Lowestoft line, you can hop on an X88 bus (konectbus.co.uk; 03300 539358) to Southwold.

Tiny Museum
Mundesley Maritime Museum, Norfolk

One of the smallest museums in the country also possesses some of the most striking views from any museum in the country. And there's a very good reason why visitors to the Mundesley Maritime Museum can enjoy such a dramatic panorama – it's housed in a former coastguard lookout post.

The petite brick building stands apart from the rest of the village of Mundesley on the northeast coast of Norfolk. Alone on the promenade it commands the beach below and the English Channel beyond. With its tiled gabled roof and smartly painted front door, it could almost pass as a miniature suburban house.

However, anyone who takes the trouble of circling the structure will quickly discover that the only windows of any size are situated right at the top and face the sea, a peculiarity that gives away the building's origins. A further clue is offered by a white-painted gaff, which is taller than the building and whose yardarm sports a pennant that can normally be relied upon to flap about in the breeze.

Step through the smartly painted door and you'll be surprised at just how much this compact little museum packs in. The ground floor takes visitors back in time to meet the people who have lived, worked and perished on this stretch of coastline. Old prints and photographs explore the day-to-day existence of those who fished the waters, ferried cargo back and forth, and crewed the local lifeboat. There's also plenty of nautical paraphernalia to scrutinise, including rocket pistols that sent distress flares into the wide

Norfolkian skies to alert the plucky lifeboatmen.

The flavour of the first floor is rather different. Visitors suddenly find themselves in a coastguard lookout of the 1930s/40s. They can examine a tide clock, view a fog horn and peruse a (not very 1930s/40s) chart table that harks back to the 17th century and the attempts to combat the activities of smugglers along the coast. There's also an agreeably old and very powerful pair of binoculars to look through, donated by a museum in Bridlington.

Although the building is not even a hundred years old it does have something of a heritage. It replaced an earlier structure that was thrown up during a period around the turn of the 19th century when the nation was in something of a febrile state. Napoleon Bonaparte was on the rampage across Europe and further afield, and an invasion by French forces, backed up by Spain, was not only feared but expected. An assiduous watch was kept on the English Channel from many locations along the coast, including Mundesley, for a fleet that never appeared over the horizon.

The current building was constructed in 1928 and just 12 years later anxious eyes again scanned the seas from Mundesley, but once again the expected invasion never materialised. After the war, the lookout post resumed its role of enabling coastguards to help protect those in the seas around the coast.

When you visit the museum you may experience a little frisson of pleasure in knowing that it's not merely preserving the local heritage but has actually gone back to performing the job for which it was built. The post became surplus to requirements as a lookout station in the early 1990s when the Coastguard Service underwent a restructuring. North Norfolk District Council snapped it up and let Mundesley Parish Council lease the building in 1994 in order to convert it into a museum. Mundesley Maritime Museum was opened the following year.

Around the same time, a charity called the National Coastwatch Institution was keen to secure a watch station in North Norfolk in order to make good a blind spot along that section of coastline. Their volunteers now staff the lookout and visitors

With its tiled gabled roof and smartly painted front door, it could almost pass as a miniature suburban house

who climb the stairs to the first floor of the museum are very likely to be greeted by one of them. They're only too happy to field questions about the radar and VHF radio they use and the life-saving work they do. The recipients of their aid include not only sailors far out to sea but also swimmers, windsurfers and individuals who ill-advisedly take to the briny on inflatable airbeds and find themselves heading out on an unplanned day trip to France.

Anyone not thrilled by tales of the sea will be pleased to learn that somehow the museum finds space for some rather surprising non-maritime exhibits. Local fossil finds are kept here, including a slice of mammoth. The story of the local railway branch line that used to run from North Walsham is also told.

In its heyday Mundesley station ran to three platforms and hosted so-called 'camping coaches' in the summer – these were specially adapted railway carriages that served as accommodation for holidaymakers. However, although the railway led to the expansion of Mundesley, the attempt to turn the little coastal village into a substantial seaside resort, though initially promising, never quite came off. The passenger service ground to a halt in 1964 and Mundesley remains a village.

The museum also provides an account of the Mundesley minefield. Laid along the seashore during World War II in order to hold up the anticipated invasion, its efficacy was all too ably demonstrated when three people were killed after wandering into it by accident. For various reasons there was a delay in clearing the minefield after the end of hostilities and two soldiers lost their lives before a clean-up operation finally got underway in 1953. It's a sobering reminder of the perils of life on the coast.

When you've had your fill of all the museum has to offer, you're in the pleasant position of not only being by the seaside but also being perfectly placed to sample the gentle charms of this modest resort that never quite made it into the big time.

Useful information

Beach Road, Mundesley, Norfolk NR11 8BG
Open Mon–Fri and Sun 11am–1pm and 2–4pm, closed Sat
Adult £1, children and concessions free
mundesleymaritimemuseum.co.uk | 01263 722068
NB The museum is manned by volunteer stewards and regrettably sometimes may not be open at the advertised hours

Getting there by public transport

As mentioned above, Mundesley railway station is sadly no more. However, North Walsham railway station is still with us – it's a stop on the Bittern line from Norwich to Sheringham. Walk the short distance from the station to Park Lane and pick up the number 5 bus (sanderscoaches. com; 01263 712800) to Mundesley High Street. Stroll along the High Street towards the sea. At the end, turn right – the museum is a short distance along Beach Road.

Tiny Theatre
The Theatre of Small Convenience, Worcestershire

Puppetry is an art form with a long and distinguished history. The first puppeteers pulled strings and manipulated figurines thousands of years ago and it appears to have been a practice that took root in many places and cultures around the world independently of each other.

Today, in countries such as the Czech Republic and Slovakia, puppetry is revered and viewed as part of the warp and weft of the respective nations' cultural identity. In Britain, if you go to the charming spa town of Great Malvern, you can also see it performed in a former toilet.

The Theatre of Small Convenience (see what they did there?) is set a little back from the pavement, behind a tree. There's a nod to crenellations on the roof. This gives it the look of a minute stone fortress, as if every Englishman's loo were his castle. And we are talking of men here because this used to be a gents. A rather fancy one, as they go. Not only is it made out of stone,

its front door is topped by a red brick archway with space for a tympanum, where a light and the theatre's name can now be found.

The shed-sized building ceased to be a toilet back in the 1980s. It was initially converted into a shop selling children's clothes. After that it became a bric-a-brac emporium. Then one day a man named Dennis Neale happened to be walking past when he noticed that the bric-a-brac shop was due to close down. Rather than shrugging and passing on, his immediate thought was – by his own recollection – 'I'd like to have a miniature theatre.' He applied to the council, the owners of the former

public convenience, and they gave him permission to transform it into a puppet theatre and charged him a peppercorn rent. The conversion took Dennis two years and he opened the doors for the first time in 1999. A new tenant took over the building in 2017 but announced plans to keep the theatre running with its founder in situ.

What Dennis and his family created is nothing short of a work of art. Inside, a wild open landscape adorns one wall, while a fantastical seascape graces another, both painted by Dennis's son. Look up and the sky above you has a huge cloud passing through it. It's not like any cloud you've ever seen before though – this one has a crowd of faces coming out of it. Elephants march around the space where a picture rail might otherwise have been. More of their fellows can be seen stomping over the cushions on the wooden chairs (which Dennis called 'the stalls'). Together with an elaborate bench ('the circle') by the door, they allow up to a dozen people to watch each show in comfort.

A large red trumpet, of the 'His Master's Voice' variety, hangs down from the ceiling, a comical mask of a man's face sits in the corner and what looks at first glance to be a mantelpiece is actually a cross-section through a piano, with all its strings on show. The decor takes its inspiration from Italian theatre and in particular the *commedia dell'arte* style, popular from the 16th to the 18th century.

This is a world of the slightly unreal, it says – where you must expect the unexpected.

The puppet theatre is no mere stage with a standard proscenium arch but resembles an intricate panelled altarpiece. Even more remarkable, it has been created out of recycled furniture gathered from far and wide. Parts of a harmonium and a violin have also been incorporated into the structure, along with the concertinaed section of an old-fashioned camera (this is later revealed to have the power of speech), the eyes of dolls and a hundred other bits and bobs. The design does not restrict itself to merely having a main stage but has various other little cavities dotted about with panels

The puppets themselves have been handcrafted by Dennis from all kinds of materials that open to allow characters to play their part in the drama. The puppets themselves have been handcrafted by Dennis from all kinds of materials, including – perhaps most surprisingly – the treadle of an old sewing machine.

After greeting visitors in his inimitable style, Dennis disappears backstage to exchange his front-of-house duties for his other role as puppet-master. All the performances – which are accompanied by music and song – last about five minutes, so each story cracks on apace. This is no endless waving about of a string of sausages à la Punch and Judy. Perhaps you'll see Titus the Too Tall Dancer or watch the tale of Captain Stradi as he sets off across the seas in a boat made of a miniature violin.

The Theatre of Small Convenience is recognised by Guinness World Records as the smallest building housing a theatre in the world. Rather charmingly, it's also a theatre run entirely for the love of puppetry – it's a strictly non-profit affair that Dennis has taken upon himself for the enjoyment it brings to both children and adults.

However, there's not just puppetry here. Since it opened, the venue has hosted plays, poetry readings, musical events, monologues and storytelling sessions. It's available for bookings, so if you fancy putting on your own show here, just give the theatre a call. No strings attached.

Useful information

Edith Walk, Malvern, Worcestershire WR14 4QH
Open Saturdays plus extra days in the school holidays – ring in advance for times | Adult £3, children £1 | wctheatre.co.uk | 01684 568933

Getting there by public transport

The theatre is just over half a mile's walk through the town from Great Malvern railway station, which is on the line between Hereford and Worcester. From the station turn left onto Avenue Road and left again when reaching Church Street. At the end turn right and then almost immediately right again into Edith Walk. NB Make sure to leave the train at Great Malvern rather than Malvern Link, the next station to the north.

24

Tiny Branch Line
Stourbridge Junction to Stourbridge Town

Tucked away at the far southwestern corner of the West Midlands – one of England's least romantically named counties – Stourbridge does not sound like the sort of place that is likely to hold a European railway record. And yet not only is that the case – the Stourbridge Junction to Stourbridge Town branch line is the shortest in the whole continent – but a 3-minute trip along its 0.8 miles of track also has the feel of a funfair ride.

For a start, there are the trains themselves. Appropriately enough, the Class 139s that ply the route are the smallest trains on Britain's rail network and have the appearance of a bus that just happens to run on rails. What's more, because they careen back and forth along a single track, they have a driving cab at both ends, making them reminiscent of Dr Dolittle's Push-Me-Pull-You.

There are just 21 seats inside with standing room for 39 further passengers, as long as those 39 are happy sacrificing their rights to

personal space. Not for nothing is the train sometimes jokily referred to as 'The Sardine Express'.

Decked out in banana yellow at the front/back and with a lime green stripe down each side (although, as with the moon, one never gets to see the far side), the Class 139 is a thoroughly modern piece of rolling stock. It's almost certainly the greenest running in Britain today as well. Made by local company Parry People Movers, it's powered by a small liquid petroleum gas engine and uses flywheel energy storage (the

flywheel captures the kinetic energy created when the train is braking then releases it when the train accelerates). This makes it exceedingly energy-efficient, particularly when attempting the incline out of Stourbridge Town station.

There are several obscure rail journeys around the country that attract very few passengers and which are kept going simply because it's cheaper to run the trains at a loss than go through all the legal rigmarole of closing the service down. The Stourbridge branch line is not one of these. Indeed, it is claimed that this is the busiest branch line for its size in the whole of Europe. Run as a shuttle service, the train makes 107 round trips every weekday (fewer at weekends) and carries over half a million passengers per year, so it wouldn't be a great surprise if it does hold the record.

You'd have thought that this continual toing and froing along the same 1,400yd of track would send both driver and conductor into a state of psychosis. Apparently not.

It is claimed that this is the busiest branch line for its size in the whole of Europe

'Anything can happen in 3 minutes,' one beaming driver told me, 'and then there's Friday night…Saturday night…It can get quite interesting.'

The service is provided by Pre Metro Operations, which boasts performance statistics that other train operating companies would tie their grandmothers to the tracks for. Some months 100% of their trains run on time. Occasionally they do have a bit of a mare with the result that the figure can slip as low as 99.5%. It means you'd be pretty unlucky to be kept waiting around, whatever train you aim to catch.

If you needed to kill time on Stourbridge Junction station, there's a buffet on the platform to soften the blow. The Caffé Presto may not exactly be a little slice of old Napoli come to the West Midlands but at least passengers can avail themselves of a cappuccino and a panino at no tremendous expense. The station it serves has two platforms, with platform 1 reserved for the exclusive use of the Stourbridge Town shuttle. A concrete trough is filled with cheery lavender plants, while a dinky little engine shed at the end of the platform looks like it's arrived fresh from the pages of *Thomas the Tank Engine*. Meanwhile, lovers of all things tiny will note with pleasure that, travelling northeast from Stourbridge Junction, the next mainline station is Lye, the shortest-named station on the national rail network.

The Stourbridge branch line was opened in 1879 by the Oxford, Worcester and Wolverhampton Railway Company. In those days, it ran from Stourbridge to a different Stourbridge Junction station which was located about 600yd to the north of the current one, so the line was even shorter than today's version. It was only in 1901 that the current Stourbridge Junction station was opened. A service has been run on the line ever since, aside from a four-year hiatus during World War I and a break of a few months in 1994 to allow Stourbridge Town station to be demolished and completely rebuilt. Diesel replaced steam in 1956 and the name of the terminus changed from Stourbridge to Stourbridge Town a year later.

Perhaps the branch line's most anxious moments came in 1964, when British Rail announced that Stourbridge Town station would be shut down, despite the fact that it had escaped being earmarked for closure in Dr Beeching's notorious report the year before. Nothing came of the announcement, but six years later the idea was floated again as a cost-cutting exercise. Once more nothing happened. Inertia is one of the great underrated virtues.

Although for most of its life the line has been double-tracked, today just a single track runs down a narrow green corridor. The colour is provided by trees and shrubs that flank the line practically its entire length, shielding passengers from suburban Stourbridge to the left and two schools to the right. Almost before its passengers know it, the train is hurtling down a slope and into Stourbridge Town station.

Built in 1994 with just a single platform, the station is endowed with a tiny ticket office, a small shelter, and a view of the spire of Our Lady and All Saints church. Conveniently, it's right next to a bus station. Built in 2012, the modern architectural design of Stourbridge Interchange renders it considerably more interesting than the vast majority of the nation's bus stations. It even features a mosaic artwork called *Cameo* by local artist Steve Field which incorporates anamorphic columns, an element of which Hans Holbein would surely have approved. Beyond, there lies Stourbridge town centre.

There's usually enough in Stourbridge to entertain visitors for several minutes at a time. A sizeable town, it made its name as an important manufacturer of glass, but the industry has dwindled to a single fully functioning factory. At the Ruskin Glass Centre, in a building that was once home to the famous Royal Doulton company, visitors can watch glass-blowing and a wide range of other glass-based craftwork taking place. However, the best time to see Stourbridge is during the British Glass Biennale, which brings together the cream of the nation's contemporary glass artists.

The day return fare between Stourbridge Junction and Stourbridge Town is less than £2. However, buy yourself a West Midlands Daytripper ticket and you can go back and forth on the line all day after 9.30am for under a tenner. If you get in around 170 trips, you're paying mere coppers per ride, making it not just one of the cheapest rail excursions in Europe but probably the cheapest on the planet.

Remarkably, the branch line is not Stourbridge's only major railway-related claim to fame. In 1829, the Stourbridge Lion, built at the local Foster, Rastrick and Co. works, became the first ever locomotive to run on a commercial line in the United States.

Getting there by public transport

Stourbridge Junction railway station lies on the Birmingham to Worcester (via Kidderminster) line. From Mon to Fri the first train from Stourbridge Junction to Stourbridge Town departs at 05.45 while the first return trip is 5 minutes later; the last train out of Stourbridge Town runs at 23.59.

On Saturdays the first/last trains run at 05.59/23.59. On Sundays the first/last trains are 09.43/19.58. (For further details see premetro.co.uk; 01384 441325)

25

Tiny County
Rutland

Multum in parvo is Rutland's jaunty motto and an apt one it is, for this is indeed a place where you'll find 'much in little'. Not only does it possess architectural riches, it's also no shirker when it comes to drowned villages and acts of civil disobedience.

Back in the early 1970s England's smallest historic county was thought so unimportant that it was actually disbanded and subsumed into Leicestershire. Not until 1997 did it manage to slough off the Leicestershirean shackles and recover its status as a county.

Today Rutland extends to 147 square miles of land, which means it could fit into Wales 54 times over if both parties were amenable to the experiment. Its paltry size is further emphasised by the fact that if you were to walk 20 miles in any one direction you would perforce leave the county – it measures just under 15 miles from north to south and less still from east to west. It has no coastline

(though, surprisingly, it does have a beach), and nothing even approaching a mountain (its highest point is a less-than-nosebleed-inducing 646ft above sea level). However, it does lay claim to a record that is all the more remarkable considering just how small the county is and how little space it has to fritter away.

Covering over 4 square miles, Rutland Water is the largest reservoir in Britain in terms of surface area. Its creation was deemed necessary because this happens to be the driest region of the UK while also being reasonably densely populated. Thus, the controversial decision was taken to flood the Gwash Valley. This entailed the destruction of the hamlet

of Nether Hambleton and most of the neighbouring village of Middle Hambleton. Work was completed in 1975 and it was flooded the following year. Only Upper Hambleton survived the deluge, sitting atop what is now a peninsula that juts into the lake, all but cutting it in twain.

Thankfully, the good people of the East Midlands and Cambridgeshire don't drink all the 4.4 billion cubic feet of water the reservoir can hold, so there's plenty left for watersports such as sailing, windsurfing and canoeing. There's also a 24-mile circular nature trail to cycle or walk around and, as of 2014, a beach created by trucking in 400 tonnes of sand. Rutland Water is an important refuge for wildlife, including numerous waterfowl such as the widgeon and tufted duck. Perhaps most exciting of all, the lake is home to England's first breeding ospreys in 150 years, making it a Mecca for birdwatchers.

If Rutland has an icon it is Normanton Church, the Corinthian-style former mausoleum that appears to have been half-submerged in the waters of the reservoir. In actual fact, when Rutland Water was created the chapel was saved from this fate by a public outcry. Instead, a layer of rubble was laid down inside and topped by concrete to raise the floor about 2ft above the maximum water level. An embankment was built around the church and a short causeway constructed so that it now forms a little headland butting into the reservoir on its southern shore. It is mostly used as a wedding venue nowadays though there is also a little museum inside telling the history of Rutland Water.

To the west of Rutland Water stands Rutland's county town, Oakham. It has a population of just under 11,000, putting it among England's smallest county towns. However, it does run to its own ancient fortress, or at least a part of one. All that is left of the Norman castle is the Great Hall, but the good news is that it is probably the most complete Norman Great Hall in England – it really is rather stunning.

The castle is also the nation's foremost repository of posh horseshoes. This came to pass due to a custom that extends back at least 500 years – namely that every peer of the realm who visits Oakham must leave a horseshoe for the Lord of the Manor. What possessed the unknown originator of this somewhat eccentric tax to impose such a levy is a mystery but their legacy can be seen covering the walls of the hall. Over 200 horseshoes are displayed, open ends down, in defiance of the folk wisdom that maintains that this causes all their luck to run out. The other remarkable thing about them is that no horse that ever lived could possibly have worn a single one, so ludicrously large are they. Most have been fashioned specifically with a visit to Oakham in mind and bear coats of arms or some fancy tracery work. Those who have submitted to the local tax include the Prince Regent (George IV), Edward VII (when Prince of Wales) and no fewer than three sitting monarchs – George VI, Elizabeth II and, back in the 1470s, Edward IV. This last, evidently not averse to the occasional act of ostentation, left the largest horseshoe of all. At about 6ft from top to bottom it dominates all the other outsized equine footwear, and makes more of a statement about Edward's insecurity (the crown was torn from him for a period and he only regained it by winning the Battle of Tewkesbury) than perhaps he would have cared to admit.

Rutland's only other town is Uppingham, which is best known for its frightfully posh £12,000-a-term boarding school founded in 1584. Alumni include E W Hornung (creator of the upper-class burglar A J Raffles) and, perhaps more surprisingly, the horror film actor Boris Karloff (real name William Pratt). The market town itself has a pleasing air of antiquity about it, as if it only grudgingly accepts that this is the 21st century.

A few miles to the northeast, near the southeastern shore of Rutland Water, lies the most eye-catchingly named village in the county: Edith Weston (though the casual peculiarity of nearby Wing runs it a close second). The village takes its moniker from Edith of Wessex, a former queen of England who was married to Edward the Confessor and who may or may not have been the guiding influence behind the creation of the Bayeux Tapestry.

Fans of bouncing bombs will want to visit Eyebrook Reservoir,

> Today, Rutland could fit into Wales 54 times over if both parties were amenable to the experiment

through whose waters the Rutland–Leicestershire border runs. In May 1943, the Lancaster bomber crews of 617 Squadron practised their skills here before carrying out attacks on the Möhne, Edersee and Sorpe dams in Germany. The so-called Dambuster Raids flooded the Ruhr Valley, killing an estimated 600 German civilians along with 1,000 forced labourers from the Soviet Union.

Finally, those who would see the county on foot are well served by the Rutland Round. This long-distance footpath which takes in Oakham and Rutland Water (twice) manages to clock up 65 miles while remaining inside the county for its entire length.

And then there's that civil disobedience. If a popular story about the people of Rutland is true, then the incorporation of the county into a Greater Leicestershire was a venture doomed from day one, or even before that. Apparently, in preparation for the amalgamation, Leicestershire County Council sent out teams to take down all the road signs that mentioned Rutland. However, the workers were nonplussed to find that the signs had already been removed.

When they began to put up new signs reflecting Leicestershire's annexation of their diminutive neighbour, the missing Rutland signs suddenly starting appearing again. This gesture of defiance was the first indication that the People's Revolutionary Front of Rutland was not to be messed with.

Useful information

Oakham Castle: Admission free | Open Mon and Wed–Sat 10am–4pm, Sun noon–4pm | oakhamcastle.org | 01572 757578

Normanton Church: For opening dates and times phone the Rutland Water Visitor Centre on 01780 686800

Getting there by public transport

Rutland's solitary railway station is at Oakham on the line between Birmingham and Peterborough. The Rutland Flyer buses (1 and 2; centrebus. info; 0116 410 5050) connect Oakham with many other parts of the county including Uppingham, while the number 9 bus (also Centrebus) runs to the Rutland Water Visitor Centre.

Tiny House
Thimble Hall, Derbyshire

Some things are tiny due to exceptional circumstances – for example, the X-craft miniature submarines (see page 240) that attacked the battleship *Tirpitz* had to be incredibly slender to slip through harbour defences, and the Theatre of Small Convenience (see page 122) is the size it is because it's restricted to the dimensions of a former gents' toilet. Thimble Hall, meanwhile, is the smallest detached house in Britain simply on account of the fact that its 18th-century builder didn't have enough money to afford a larger plot.

The unknown villager clearly didn't have much money for the house either, because it measures just 11ft 10in by 10ft 3in and is a mere 12ft 2in tall. Like Quay House (see page 219), it's a one-up, one-down affair, with a ladder joining the two rooms (both a cosy 8ft 1in by 7ft 1in). However, unlike the minuscule Welsh property, Thimble Hall doesn't even have the benefit of running water. A bathroom and kitchen are luxuries never seen here. In 1756, the year it was built, such things perhaps mattered a little

less. In any case, the village fountain was constructed just outside in 1823 (it's still there today) so at least, after that year, successive owners wouldn't have had to traipse hither and yon to collect water.

As it happens, the building didn't always remain a house. It's known to have seen life as an antiques shop, a butcher's and a cobbler's. It was last used for domestic purposes back in the 1930s. A family of eight are reputed to have lived in it shortly before then, which doesn't really

bear thinking about. The Grade II listed building is in the attractive Peak District village of Youlgreave (often also spelled Youlgrave – it's probably best not to ask the locals about this unless you enjoy heated discussions), which is located in the area known as White Peak. The River Bradford curls around its southern border, while the limestone dales that surround the village are very popular with walkers. The house itself is in the vernacular style and would not stand out from its handsome fellows at all were it not for its size. Constructed of creamy limestone, it has just two small windows in its front aspect and a rustic lintel over a rather petite door. A flag-tiled roof supports a suspiciously modern-looking chimney stack.

After its abandonment, the house fell into a state of decrepitude and might have become a ruin had it not been put up for auction in 1999. It was bought by Bruno Frederick, the famous Chesterfield ice cream magnate. If the rumours are true, he fought off spoon-bending maverick Uri Geller and bidders from around the world to land the house for £39,500, way over the £5,000–£15,000 guide price. It does make one nostalgic for those not-so-far-off happy days when a house might have feasibly sold for £5,000–£15,000

> It's known to have seen life as an antiques shop, a butcher's and a cobbler's

rather than 30 times that amount. Even so, paying the best part of £40,000 for about 115 square feet of non-habitable property does seem like a leap of faith. There's clearly money in ice cream. The Frederick's family legend has it that the company's Italian founder walked all the way to Sheffield from Parma in 1875 to bring frozen milk products to the masses. He was evidently rather good at it and the successful business has been passed down the generations ever since, a tradition that may have deprived Youlgreave of the honour of hosting the international headquarters of the Uri Geller School of Psychokinesis.

At last, nearly two decades after being purchased, something is happening at Thimble Hall. The Frederick family has decided to turn it into 'a display case for a collection of thimbles' (one can see their thinking there). They also have plans to mount rolling exhibitions of locally produced arts and crafts. Rather more ambitiously, in 2017 Bruno's son Jonathan announced that the family was seeking planning permission to turn the premises into a boutique hotel – unsurprisingly the smallest in the land – for which they would commission appropriately scaled-down furniture. It means that very soon you may not only be able to feast your eyes upon what is purported to be the world's largest collection of thimbles, but you may be able to sleep with them too. As life experiences go, that will probably be a first for most people.

Useful information

Moor Lane, Youlgreave, Derbyshire DE45 1US
Opening sometime in 2018 – check website for details
thimblehall.co.uk | 01246 275293

Getting there by public transport

There are two good options. If you don't want to change buses, you can head for Matlock railway station, the terminus of a line from Derby, and time your arrival to coincide with the infrequent number 172 bus (hulleys-of-baslow.co.uk; 01246 582246) from stand 2 at the Interchange. That will take you to Holywell Lane in Youlgreave in about 50 minutes.

Alternatively, you can pick up a more frequent service to Haddon Hall (on the road to Bakewell) such as the Transpeak bus (highpeakbuses.com; 0116 410 5050), which connects with the 171 (Hulleys again) to Youlgreave. The house is on a triangle (with the aforementioned fountain in the middle of it) at the junction of Church Street and Moor Lane near the centre of the village.

Tiny Museum
Warley Museum, West Yorkshire

There are some record-breaking attractions – particularly of the smallest/tallest/biggest variety – that come into being with the sole purpose of breaking a record and then reaping the rewards in publicity and, if all goes according to plan, cold hard lucre.

There are others that are born out of inspiration, love and dedication and then just happen to find themselves at one extreme of the spectrum in their particular category. Warley Museum, the smallest one in Britain, is very much in the second camp.

It's also one of Britain's newest museums. In 2016, under the aegis of British Telecom's Adopt-a-Kiosk scheme, the Warley Community Association (WCA) decided to take on a rather forlorn and seldom-used telephone box outside the Maypole Inn in the centre of town. The pros and cons of turning it into a library or a station for a defibrillator were duly discussed. Telephone boxes are not known for their palatial interiors but the committee members eventually voted to transform theirs into a museum about the town (which, to be fair, is the size of a large village). They at once put out a call for donations that would help tell the story of the area.

Warley is an ancient village: it goes back to the Domesday Book – in which it gets a mention – and before. The father of the Brontë sisters lived there for a while and for many years it was the home of much-loved Yorkshireman Wilfred Pickles – the first radio presenter on the BBC to speak with a regional accent rather than in received pronunciation.

The WCA's own Eliana Bailey and Kathryn Gallagher were selected to make the project happen. A joiner named Doug Bailey renovated the box, stripping it down from top to bottom before refitting it and giving it an overdue coat of paint.

The museum was then curated by Chris and Paul Czainski, both much feted and exhibited artists from nearby Luddenden. Paul Czainski, who specialises in *trompe l'œil*, etched the panels of glass with depictions of Warley's history and created an illustrated board for the back of the box that displays brief biographies of the 'Notables of Warley Parish'. Chris Czainski, meanwhile, set to work on a mosaic floor comprising broken pottery and *objets trouvés* from Warley's gardens.

To much fanfare, Warley Museum was opened on Saturday 8 October 2016 by the Mayor and Mayoress of Calderdale. A brass band played and morris dancers danced. The first exhibits included antique jewellery, a perfume atomiser, whistles and myriad other domestic items from Warley's past.

Like any museum worth its salt, the smallest museum in Britain (and possibly even the world – an application to the Guinness World Records has now been made) is not content to show the same exhibits ad infinitum, so every few months the display is changed. The new exhibits are placed in transparent boxes attached to the window panels so that they can be seen from both inside and outside.

On the afternoon of Sunday 8 October 2017, a celebration of the first anniversary of Warley Museum was held outside the Maypole Inn. It was attended by the new Mayor and Mayoress of Calderdale; a specially commissioned poem was read by poet Aunt Grizelda; and music was provided by a local brass ensemble called the Friendly Band (they're not necessarily friendly, they're simply based in a village of that name) and folk combo The Landlubbers.

Assuming every anniversary of the museum is to be commemorated,

> Telephone boxes are not known for their palatial interiors but the committee members voted to turn theirs into a museum

8 October (or the nearest weekend day to that date if the WCA decide to bend the rules a little) is a good time to go along if you like a bit of a knees-up when you visit a museum.

Otherwise, at any other time of the year the good people of Warley are more than happy for you to have a quiet browse around the museum of which they are justly proud.

Useful information

Warley Museum: Beside the Maypole Inn (details below) | Open daily 8am–4pm (when closed many of the exhibits can be viewed from the outside) Admission free | warleyca.co.uk/warley-museum

Maypole Inn: 32–34 Warley Town Lane, Warley, Halifax, West Yorkshire HX2 7RZ | Open Mon 5–11pm, Tue–Thu noon–3pm and 5–11pm, Fri–Sat noon–midnight, Sun noon–10.30pm |Food served Tue–Thu noon–2.30pm and 5.30–8.30pm, Fri–Sat noon–2.30pm and 5.30–9pm, Sun noon–7.30pm maypole.jimdo.com | 01422 835861

Getting there by public transport

Warley Town Lane, in the centre of Warley, is a 1½-mile walk from Sowerby Bridge railway station, on the Calder Valley line between Leeds and Manchester. From the station, follow Station Road down to Town Hall Street, which becomes Wharf Street. Turn left into Tuel Lane and where it ends turn left along Burnley Road. Cross the road carefully and, almost immediately, turn right into Blackwall Lane. Where this forks, bear right. This is Water Hill Lane which becomes Cliff Hill Lane and leads to Warley Town Lane. The museum is next to the Maypole Inn.

28

Tiny Canal
Ulverston Canal, Cumbria

The waterway at Ulverston is not your usual canal. For a start, even for a canal, it's prodigiously straight, a veritable Roman road untainted by kinks or deviations from one end to the other. Just a single lock complicates its journey from town to sea, and that is only necessary to spare it from the effects of the tides. Furthermore, at just 1¼ miles long, it's but a little stick of blue on the map, as if it had been extracted deliberately from the jack-straws jumble of the nation's canal network and placed carefully to one side.

It should be said that this is not Britain's shortest canal, as is sometimes claimed. That honour resides with the Wardle Lock branch of the Trent and Mersey Canal in Middlewich, Cheshire. That one is a mere tiddler: just 154ft long, with almost half of that taken up with a lock. However, when the Ulverston Canal opened in 1796, it was indeed the shortest one the nation had ever seen. It was also the widest (66ft) and the deepest (15ft), although it was later trumped in both these

departments by the Manchester Ship Canal. It does still maintain the record for being Britain's straightest canal though – a title it's unlikely ever to lose.

Although it was evidently not one of the great civil engineering undertakings of the time, it did provide a very simple and effective solution to a problem. This involved the difficulties of tides, Ulverston's location, and the town's need to ship coal in and slate and iron out. Ulverston had become a major trading centre by the 18th century but it was a mile or so inland from Morecambe Bay and the ships and boats that serviced the town had to load and unload their cargoes some distance from where they were needed. Docking was also a difficulty with the immense difference between high and low tide in the bay.

A meeting of interested parties held in 1791 provided the stimulus for a canal that would link the town with the coast. It would be wide enough to allow plentiful shipping on it and deep enough to accommodate the draughts of heavily laden vessels. Two years later, an act of parliament giving the canal the go-ahead received royal assent. There was no time to lose and the canal was completed in a commendably speedy three years. However, it did cost around £9,000 (roughly equivalent to forking out £67m today), which was three times over budget.

The new canal attracted industry and in the early 1800s mills and factories opened up around it. These boosted further the amount of coal required in the town and the canal was soon alive with incoming colliers. All seemed to be functioning well. Unfortunately, there were still the vicissitudes of the sea to be reckoned with. In December 1808, a terrible storm racked the west coast of Britain from Liverpool all the way up to Stranraer.

In the aftermath, the *Lancaster Gazette* published a sombre report on the tragedy in which dozens of ships were lost:

> *On Friday evening a gale of wind came on from the westward which caused great damage to the coasting vessels of Preston. The JENNY (Capt. Iddon) laden with coal for Ulverston was driven on Horse Bank and went to pieces, the crew lost. The ELLEN AND SUSAN (Captain Rymer) laden with coal for Ulverston was lost on the Meols coast. The BETTY AND MARY (Captain Sharples) for Ulverston, stranded about two miles below Lytham. The ENGINE (Captain Ashworth) laden with coal for Ulverston, supposed to be totally lost with all her crew. The AGNES (Captain Muncaster) for Ulverston is supposed to be lost, as her boat was taken up near Blackpool. The LION (Captain Sumner) with coal for Ulverston was stranded near Blackpool and much damaged, crew saved.*

As local historian Jennifer Snell observes:

Those small, almost certainly elderly vessels which were to be seen regularly in Ulverston canal plying to and fro carrying coal for the town fared worst, and until replacements were found Ulverston must have endured a "fuel famine" over the Christmas and New Year period.

The canal head is a quiet place nowadays. Beside the basin there's a store that sells building and agricultural supplies but otherwise it feels like the town has turned its back on the canal, which in many ways it has. At least there's a footpath along the entire northern bank, so you can walk the canal from the town end to the sea. Right at the start you'll find an innovative but simple map of the canal. It takes the form of a steel sheet with a slit cut right through it to represent the canal and a few other features highlighted in relief. The first of these is a railway line.

Cut off from the east by the Cumbrian mountains, Ulverston was reached by the railway from the west in 1854. The line pushed tentatively a little further east three years later. The Six Arches Bridge had to be built for this extension and as you walk down the canal path you'll pass under it.

As you do you might like to reflect on the symbolism of the tracks flying over the water, for the railway was largely responsible for the demise of the canal as a commercial venture. It petered out in 1916 and was abandoned completely in 1945. But in its heyday, this area around the canal head and the basin just the other side of the bridge was alive with industry. There were not only ironworks but also a paper mill, a timber yard, a foundry, a gas works and several shipyards, among other ventures.

Just over halfway along the canal you'll reach the rolling bridge, built in the early 1880s and the only one of its type left in England. This too used to carry railway tracks over the canal – for both an ironworks and a little branch line to Bardsea, a few miles down the coast. It was a clever piece of technology: a crossing that was hydraulically powered so that it could be pulled back across to the south side of the canal in order to allow shipping to pass. The line to Bardsea is long gone but the bridge carried rail traffic to a factory owned by GlaxoSmithKline up until 1994. Sadly the bridge has been locked into position but there is a pedestrian

walkway now, so you can wander onto it to take in views of the canal.

And so to the canal foot, where the waterway ends as abruptly as it began. A stone jetty can still be seen here, along with another basin, some mooring rings on the shoreline, and some stout wooden lock gates that prevented the canal's water from escaping into the sea. The inner gate has been reduced to a mere skeleton but the one facing Morecambe Bay is still doing its job of keeping the canal filled.

That same Morecambe Bay provides a spectacular finale to this short journey along the canal. The deep golden Cartmel Sands are spread out before you with the extraordinary Leven railway viaduct skimming low across them to the north. To the south lies Chapel Island, once eulogised by Wordsworth. The chapel ruins you may be able to pick out are fake. They were put there by a retired colonel in the 1820s to make the view from his house on the coast more picturesque.

For many years the canal foot was the home of Schollick's Shipyard. The last boat built here was an elegant schooner. It was named *Hearts of Oak* on account of the fact that it was constructed of oak left lying around at a shipyard in Barrow after it closed down. It was launched in 1912 and served as a pilot boat for Ulverston Canal until 1938 when the ironworks closed. During the war it became a rescue boat, and helped pluck several downed airmen from the sea. It is still sailed around Morecambe Bay so it's worth looking out for its three distinctive russet sails as it single-handedly keeps the spirit of the canal alive on the waters.

Useful information

Always open | Admission free | To help preserve the canal, contact the award-winning Ulverston Canal Regeneration Group at ulverstoncrg.co.uk

Bay Horse Hotel: A 17th-century former coaching inn at the canal foot. Open for lunch and dinner | thebayhorsehotel.co.uk | 01229 583972

Getting there by public transport

From Ulverston railway station, on the Furness line from Lancaster to Barrow-in-Furness, it's a walk of about a mile along County Road and Canal Street to the canal head.

Tiny Station
Ribblehead Station, North Yorkshire

High up on the B6255, a road that bravely attempts to cross some particularly brooding and weather-scoured Yorkshire hills, you'll encounter one of the most glorious viaducts in England.

Nearby, a stony track leads up a slope to a trim Victorian building. It would seem a nonsensical place to build a house. It's in the middle of nowhere, 6 miles from the village its address purports to be near, and horribly exposed to the elements (and this is the self-styled God's Own County, where the elements, terrified of being thought 'soft', deliver up a near constant barrage of horizontal rain). But take a closer look and you'll see that this is a former stationmaster's house and that behind it there's a little station commanding one of the finest views you'll see from a railway platform.

Like the Yorkshire Dales National Park that lies around it, Ribblehead station is a thing of beauty. Sitting proudly on the notoriously scenic Settle to Carlisle line, it has now been completely restored to its Victorian grandeur.

It's something that's said many times about many places, but when you step out of the train and are left alone on the platform, it really does feel like you've been transported into the past. Crimson-painted lamp posts line the platforms; tubs of flowers bring their own splashes of colour; a clock ('W Potts & Sons, Leeds') ticks away the minutes until the next train; old signs advertise the delights of 'Ingleton – Beauty Spot of the North – First Turn Left'; and the many-gabled station building is as spick and span as the day it was opened.

That day was 4 December 1876. But there was no 'I hereby declare

Ribblehead station open' because the first name the stop went by was Batty Green. The inspiration for it came from a nearby stream, which had garnered its curious nomenclature because a man with the surname Batty had drowned his wife in it. We've the Reverend E H Woodall of Settle to thank for the fact that the station is no longer named after a murderer. He sent a letter to the Midland Railway Company with the suggestion that the station be called Ribblehead instead, and on 1 May 1877 the nameboards were duly changed.

However, it's something of a mystery as to why there should be a station here at all. There were no plans to site one by the viaduct originally. Then, as now, there were very few people living in the area and those who did were to be served by a station at Selside, a hamlet on the line to the south. But in the year before the line opened, someone at the Midland Railway Company decided to rob Selside of its station and open one here instead. The only plausible reason for doing so would have been to make life marginally easier for the people of Ingleton and Hawes (10 miles away in the other direction), but there's no knowing what the actual rationale behind it was.

Ribblehead never did get used a great deal – at least not for the purpose for which it was intended. Shortly after the station opened, the waiting room began to be used as a surrogate church by the vicar of St Mary's in Ingleton. He held services in the little space with hymns sung to the strains of a harmonium. Come the late 1930s and the station's exposure to the weather made it an ideal spot for siting a Ministry of Defence meteorological station. Special training had to be given to station staff so that they could take readings from the equipment and transmit them in code to the MoD. The station still serves a meteorological function today, as home to an automatic weather station.

> We've the Reverend E H Woodall of Settle to thank for the fact that the station is no longer named after a murderer

Despite this activity, it came as no real surprise when, in 1970, the station was closed down. It might never have opened again had British Rail had its way, because in the 1980s the company declared that it was going to close the entire route from Settle to Carlisle. The line was only saved by the work of a hurriedly formed campaigning group.

Meanwhile, at Ribblehead, the northbound platform had been demolished to make room for sidings used by a local quarry. It meant that when the decision was taken in 1986 to re-open the station, a new platform for northbound trains had to be built. Since the sidings were still in use, space was eventually found for it further along the line, which explains why today the station has a curious lopsided look. There's nowt fancy like a footbridge or a subway linking the platforms so passengers are obliged to change from one to the other by what is known in railway parlance as a 'barrow crossing'. The dips between the platforms, the tracks and the rails have been filled in to make a path for pedestrians that doesn't impede the trains.

The station was in a dilapidated state though – a wreck of a place battered by a century of harsh weather and decades of neglect.

Its saviour came in the form of a voluntary organisation called the Settle and Carlisle Railway Trust which took a 125-year lease on the station in 1999. Not only did the members of this organisation make Ribblehead a place of wonder once more, they also created a visitor centre in the former booking office and hall, slipped in a tiny buffet bar, and transformed the porters' room into a little shop.

The visitor centre now houses a museum that tells the story not only of the station but also of the Ribblehead Viaduct and the methods used in digging railway tunnels.

Outside, on the platforms, both the wind and the panorama are breathtaking. From here you can see all of the Yorkshire Three Peaks. Pen-y-ghent dominates the backdrop to the east; to the south, lurking behind Park Fell, is the hulking mass of Ingleborough; while to the west is the mighty ridge of Whernside, along whose lower slopes the line runs. From the far western end of the main platform you can also catch a sidelong look at the Ribblehead Viaduct. For those not taking on the Yorkshire Three Peaks Challenge (a 24-mile walk that includes the three summits and must be completed in under 12 hours), a new exhibit in the

visitor centre allows guests to explore all three peaks (and the viaduct) in virtual form.

The history of this station's section of the Settle to Carlisle line says a great deal about Victorian Britain. Work began around 1870 on overcoming two major obstacles:

a hill called Blea Moor and a dale called Low Sleights. The solutions proposed were a tunnel and a viaduct respectively. It was typical of the Victorians that they managed to pull off two engineering miracles in the creation of the 1½-mile Blea Moor Tunnel and the 440yd Ribblehead

of infrastructure and of their families. Around 215 people gave their lives so that trains could pass through this slice of challenging topography. Many died in what were then deemed 'inevitable' worksite accidents – it was just part and parcel of building a railway line. What is even more shocking is that over half the fatalities were babies and small children. Their short lives were snuffed out by diseases such as smallpox that they contracted in the nearby shanty towns where the navvies lived with their dependants. So extreme was the death toll that the corpses of the victims completely filled up the local churchyard in Chapel-le-Dale. The cemetery at St Leonard's had to be expanded on donated land in order to accommodate the incessant flow of coffins, no matter that most of them did not take up much room. If you visit the churchyard today – it's just 2 miles along the road towards Ingleton – you'll notice something rather chilling. The families of the men who built the tunnel and the viaduct were so poor that not one of the graves of their dead has a headstone.

Viaduct. The latter is also a joy to behold and has become one of the most photographed stretches of railway line anywhere in the country.

It was also typical of the Victorians that there was a scandalous lack of attention paid to the wellbeing of the men who built these essential pieces

But to happier things. It's now possible to experience something of what it must have been like to live and work at Ribblehead station. The Settle and Carlisle Railway Trust not only breathed new life into the place but they also bought up the derelict stationmaster's house next door, restored it (winning an award in the process) and converted it into a smart holiday let.

Despite the fact that the station has been left stranded in the middle of nowhere, it does have a companion. As improbable as it may seem, opposite the point where the track leads up to Ribblehead there's a cosy pub in an old stone building called The Station Inn. If you stay at the stationmaster's house, you will not only be perfectly placed for forays up and down the Settle to Carlisle line, you'll also have one of the most unlikely of locals on your doorstep.

Useful information

Visitor centre open Apr–Oct daily 10.15am–3.15pm ('sometimes later'), staffed by volunteers | Admission free (donations welcome) | For more information, or to book a stay in the stationmaster's house (sleeps 4+2), visit sandctrust.org.uk | 01768 800208

Reports from the automatic weather station at Ribblehead can be found at mylocalweather.org.uk/ribblehead

The Station Inn: Newly refurbished pub, rooms and bunk barn | Open daily 11am–midnight | Food served Mon–Fri noon–2.30pm and 6–8.45pm, Sat–Sun and bank holidays 12–8.45pm
stationinnribblehead.co.uk | 01524 241274

Getting there by public transport

Ribblehead station is on the Settle to Carlisle line. Trains head north for Carlisle and south to Leeds every couple of hours.
(northernrailway.co.uk)

30

Tiny River
River Bain, North Yorkshire

The shortest river in England that possesses a name, the River Bain, somehow manages to pack all kinds of pleasurable experiences into its 2½-mile run down a largely overlooked valley in the Yorkshire Dales National Park.

Tipping out of Semer Water, Yorkshire's second largest natural lake, it flows away from the hamlet of Countersett heading northeast to carve out a valley to the east of Semerdale Hall. It is flanked for a while by Gilledge Wood before hurtling on to Bainbridge where it serves as a natural barrier between the village and the remains of a Roman fort. Almost immediately afterwards the Bain plunges into Wensleydale and the River Ure, its eventful journey all too soon brought to an end.

It's remarkable to reflect that, in a county as sizeable as Yorkshire, a lake that is just half a mile long and covers a mere 100 acres should be its second

largest. Only Malham Tarn, to the northeast of Settle, is more expansive than Semer Water. The lake that gives birth to the Bain is popular with water sports enthusiasts and is a highlight for hikers walking the curiously named A Pennine Journey long-distance footpath. Its beauty did not go unnoticed by J M W Turner, who came here in July 1816 and made several sketches and paintings of it.

Linguists, on the other hand, get excited about Semer Water for quite a different reason: its name is pleonastic (i.e. it repeats itself). There are a number of examples of geographical features in Britain where this occurs, the most famous being the eight separate British waterways bearing the name River Avon. (Avon derives from the Welsh *afon*, meaning 'river', so the River Avon actually means River River.) Semer Water is a rare triple version of the form: 'Se' derives from the Old English sæ, which means 'lake'; 'mer' is a shortening of mere, which also means lake (as seen in Windermere, Grasmere etc.); while 'water' is clearly a third reference to the fact that it is a lake. In fairness, it doesn't take all that much to excite a linguist.

The lake is also the subject of a local legend. The story goes that there was once a prosperous town on the spot where Semer Water now sits and that it was visited by an elderly man who called from door to door begging for something to eat and drink. He was refused by everyone until he came to a hovel on the hillside on the outskirts of the town. Here a woman and her husband, though paupers themselves, invited the man in and shared what little they had with him. On leaving them, the elderly man is said to have uttered a curse on the town. He bade Semer Water to rise up and sink the place, all except for the lowly house where he was offered hospitality. As is often the case with such tales, the words of the curse came to pass – the town was inundated and the hovel spared.

The Bain begins to leave Countersett behind as soon as the nascent river flows out of Semer Water. Back in the 17th century, the isolation of the compact hamlet made it ideal as a location for illicit religious gatherings. Outlawed Quakers met in a stone manor house called Countersett Hall, far from the prying eyes of those who might inform on them.

Also to the west of the river is Semerdale Hall, now a 500-acre dairy and sheep farm but once a manor house and estate belonging to a family called Coates. A little further downstream comes steeply shelving Gilledge Wood overlooking the river's one island, a nameless little finger of land.

The only major centre of population on the Bain is Bainbridge, named after its venerable river crossing. The Romans, however, knew the place as Virosidum ('the settlement of true men') and the 2-acre fort they built beside the Bain can be seen to the east on Brough

Hill. Virosidum was probably built by Quintus Petillius Cerialis during his governorship of Britain (c. AD 71–74) to aid the campaigns waged against a powerful Celtic tribe called the Brigantes. The fort was at the northern apex of a triangle of Roman roads, an outpost established deep in the heart of Brigantian territory. Set out in a parallelogram, there are entrances to the fort in the centre of each of the sides, as was the Roman custom. The rampart, defended in three directions by a double-ditch system, was once 20ft wide with a wooden parapet on top.

The fort was still in use in the early 5th century, when it was mentioned in the *Notitia Dignitatum*, a document that listed the thousands of administrative offices, army units and forts that made up the Roman Empire. In the early 3rd century the defences had been overhauled, with a stone facing being added to the rampart by the Sixth Cohort of Nervians. These were auxiliary soldiers from the Nervii tribe in the province of Gallia Belgica (located in modern-day Belgium,

Luxembourg and the Netherlands). They had thrown in their lot with the Romans, who had formed them into cohorts and sent them out to help maintain the Empire's grip on western Europe.

Virosidum's garrison eventually abandoned the place and when the Domesday Book came to be written there was nothing there but forest. A manor and a scattering of small houses in the 12th century gave birth to the village of 'Beyntbrigg' and the building of homes for foresters expanded it further. Today, nearly 500 people call the village home, and although there are few really ancient buildings left, Bainbridge does possess a rare gem in the Rose and Crown. The inn has slaked the thirst of the local populace and weary travellers since 1445, making it one of Yorkshire's oldest pubs. An ancient horn is kept there and sounded every night at 10pm between the Feast of Holy Rood (27 September) and Shrove Tuesday. In days of yore, the same horn was

Pleasingly, it's possible to walk the greater part of England's shortest named river on footpaths blown to guide foresters through the surrounding woodland to the safety of the village.

But the Bain has a very important date with the Ure and it hurries under the bridge, past the Quaker meeting house, and in a trice has flowed beyond Bainbridge.

The river's haste has been harnessed by the local people since the first hydroelectric scheme was installed here towards the end of Victoria's reign. Nowadays, the river produces electricity for 40 houses in the village. Having done this good deed, the Bain adds its strength to the River Ure a mile or so to the west of the picturesque village of Askrigg.

Pleasingly, it's possible to walk the greater part of England's shortest named river on footpaths. From the northern tip of Semer Water, a path on the north side of the Bain leads quickly to a minor road. Use this to cross the river and a signpost for A Pennine Journey will guide you along the riverbank before climbing 160ft or so to run parallel with the Bain all the way to the outskirts of Bainbridge. From there you cross the eponymous bridge, which carries the A684 over the waters, and take the first right to continue following the river to a crossing called Yorebridge just to the west of the point where the Bain flows into the Ure.

Getting there by public transport

First off, don't make the mistake of confusing it with the other River Bain, a rather longer affair that flows through Lincolnshire. Instead, head for Darlington railway station, take the X26 bus (arrivabus.co.uk/north-east) to Catterick Garrison, and then the 156 bus (littlewhitebus.co.uk; 01969 667400) to Bainbridge, the village at the northern end of the River Bain.

On Sundays, you can go to Northallerton railway station and take the number 856 bus (dalesbus.org/LWB Voyager.pdf; 01677 425203) direct to Bainbridge.

Tiny Bridge
Ashness Bridge, Cumbria

Once upon a time, before the motorway and the railway, before the turnpike and the canal, there was the packhorse route. From the early Middle Ages right up until the 18th century, when vast improvements were made to the nation's major roads, the intricate pattern of packhorse tracks provided the network by which goods could travel, tied securely onto a beast of burden.

Ashness Bridge lay on such a packhorse route and was built to convey humans and animals across a stream called Barrow Beck that flows down into Derwent Water from a mountain called High Seat. A small and apparently insignificant bridge, it has just a single span made of local stone and slate, and was probably a replacement for an earlier bridge.

A few strides are all that is necessary to pass from one side to the other, making it one of the nation's smaller Grade II listed buildings. However, trifling though it be, there's a very good reason why Ashness Bridge is worth visiting, and we'll come on to that in a moment.

Some of the most important packhorse tracks were metalled in some way, often with flagstones, particularly if they were routes put to use by some prosperous monastery or member of the nobility. In Cumbria, where these tracks were commonly known as trods, the paths would climb over mountain passes, as they made their way from valley to valley by the most favourable route. These tracks only had to be as wide as a single horse or pony. If more than one animal was being led, they simply followed one behind the

other, with sometimes as many as 25 horses forming a great convoy of commodities. Vast quantities of slate from the mines high up at Honister were transported down to the coast this way to be shipped off around the world. Imports coming through Whitehaven harbour, such as tobacco and spirits, would make journeys along the tracks to towns inland or the snuff mill at Kendal.

Mountains weren't the only obstacles the packhorses and their guides had to overcome. The Lake District is a place suffused with streams and rivers – a complicated lattice spread over the whole area – and each one had to be forded or crossed by a bridge. Of course, constructing bridges cost money – especially ones strong enough to take the weight of fully laden horses – and so no money was wasted in building them wider than they needed to be. Although not every narrow stone bridge one comes across is necessarily a packhorse bridge, there is at least a fair chance that it might be. Ashness Bridge certainly was one. It was built sometime in the 18th century with a parapet added later.

The ancient counties of Cumberland and Westmorland (equivalent to most of today's Cumbria) were not only two of the poorer regions of England, their rugged terrain rendered them two of the most isolated as well. Furthermore, until relatively recently, the English viewed mountains with an amount of dread – they were dangerous places to be avoided rather than enjoyed. For these reasons, the progress in road communication that had taken place in the rest of the country was slower to materialise in this far northwest corner. Hence, there was still a need to build new packhorse bridges such as Ashness as late as the 18th century.

The crossing had to be significantly widened in the 20th century in order to allow cars to pass over it (but only then in single file and with caution). Today, those cars can follow the trail only as far as the cluster of houses at

Watendlath, where the road comes to a halt. The path continues over another attractive packhorse bridge. It's unclear whether the packhorse track ended in Watendlath, continued down to Rosthwaite, or perhaps even climbed steeply where today the bridleway snakes its way southeastward from pass to pass before plunging down to the southern end of Thirlmere.

You can follow the trail yourself if you fancy a good hike (and you come prepared, of course). However, before you head off, you'd be advised to stop a while by Ashness Bridge and look up. The Lake District is rightly famed for its sumptuously rich vistas, but the view from this bridge just happens to be one of the most treasured of all. From this eyrie you can gaze across Borrowdale with its handsome oak trees. These so-called Atlantic Oakwoods are one of Britain's scattered little pockets of temperate rainforest and are home to woodpeckers, flycatchers and red

A few strides are all that is necessary to pass from one side to the other, making it one of the nation's smaller listed buildings

and roe deer. Beyond the trees lies Derwent Water, a wonderful splash of cobalt blue if you come up when the heavens are clear. The little town of Keswick sits on the mere's far shore, while behind it rises Skiddaw, one of the Lake District's highest peaks. Seen from this angle, the colossal mountain seems to be spreading its arms gently around the lake. The scene has been painted, sketched, drawn and photographed countless times, beautified by this aesthetically pleasing little humpback of stone in the foreground.

Next to the road, just below the bridge, you'll find a memorial to one of the all-time great Lake District fell runners. This is the Bob Graham cairn, a humble little finger of stones. A brass plate records his greatest feat: 'In memory of Robert Graham of Keswick (1889–1966), who on the 13–14 June 1932 traversed 42 Lakeland peaks within 24 hours, a record which stood for 28 years.'

In carrying off this astonishing show of athletic prowess, he covered

66 miles and climbed nearly 27,000ft. The name of this rather remarkable guesthouse owner lives on in the Bob Graham Round, one of the blue riband events in the world of fell running. It's a simple enough challenge – to have 'done' the Round, all you need to do is complete the same route inside 24 hours.

If that feels like something you might put off for a year or two to give that hamstring injury a real chance to heal, you could instead walk half a mile or so further up the road from the bridge, following the packhorse trail, to Surprise View. Without wishing to spoil the surprise, this spot offers up another prized Lakeland panorama, with views all the way to Scotland if the weather is playing ball. Alternatively, you could take the footpath that leads off from the bridge to follow Barrow Beck up to the waterfall on Ashness Gill. The path then leaves the beck to reach the summit of High Seat, where yet more eye-pleasing vistas await.

Finally, do keep your eyes on the trees in these parts, for this is one of the last outposts of the red squirrel on mainland England. And who doesn't love a red squirrel?

Useful information

Watendlath road, off B5289, above Derwent Water, Cumbria
Always open | Admission free | nationaltrust.org.uk

Getting there by public transport

From Penrith railway station, walk to the bus station where you'll find an X4 bus to take you to Keswick. There you can change onto a 78 bus (both stagecoachbus.com; 01539 722143) for the short journey along Derwent Water, leaping off gazelle-like at Ashness Gate, the landing stage at Barrow Bay, to walk the few hundred yards up the minor road that leads off the main B5289 and crosses Ashness Bridge. Better still, arrive in style by taking the ferry from Keswick along Derwent Water to the Ashness Gate landing stage and follow the same route to the bridge (keswick-launch.co.uk; 017687 72263)

Tiny Museum
The Ferry Hut, Alnmouth, Northumberland

There's nothing quite like an estuary for making one think of the word 'lazy'. The waters at this late stage of a river have lost their youthful vigour and, perhaps out of trepidation or simple old age, are not in any hurry to disgorge themselves into the rough and tumble of the sea.

Only an incoming tide might produce anything that might be described as hurried, as waters that have perhaps travelled across an entire ocean flow upstream inquisitively, knowing that their time on land is short, like tourists put aground off a newly docked cruise liner that must set sail again before sundown.

But lazy is not a word that would spring to mind at all if one were to witness a ferryman straining at the oars as he conveyed his passengers across the Aln Estuary. Sadly, it's not a sight that has been seen there these 50 years. Today, although there are plenty of small craft along the bank of the estuary and fishing boats

among them too, you'll search in vain for a ferry.

There is, however, a ferryman's hut. Or at least a former ferryman's hut. As if to prove that we live in a world in which more or less anything can be turned into something else, no matter how unlikely, here is a ferryman's hut that is now a museum. Aside from the fact that, as a general rule, museums are good things and provide society with a vital cultural and educational pillar that helps people understand who they are and where they've come from, the Ferry Hut (sometimes more grandly called the Ferryman's Hut Museum) serves another very useful purpose: without it, who but

a scholarly elite would know that ferrymen's huts were a thing?

And yet it stands to reason that those doughty men and women who guide us dutifully across the waves (see page 109) must have somewhere to shelter from the elements when not shuttling us back and forth, and where better to do that than in a hut? And up on the coast of Northumberland they're rarely short of elements from which to shelter. No doubt the men who rowed their passengers across the River Aln, which can become quite wide at the point where the hut stands, were only too glad to have somewhere warm to dry themselves off.

The last Aln ferryman to do so was called John Brown. He was a former miner and fisherman and rowed a large boat that could carry up to six people. Like the many ferrymen before him, he had to seek permission from the Duke of Northumberland to operate a fee-charging service across the estuary. The fare depended on the tide. If it happened to be out, passengers paid 2d. However, if the tide was in, the price increased to 3d because it was so much further for the ferryman to row. The thrifty traveller thus timed their movements according to the tides when possible.

John Brown retired back in the 1960s. Since then, anyone wishing to cross the Aln has either had to do so in their own vessel or press on upstream to the nearest bridge, to the west of Alnmouth, which nowadays carries the B1338 safely across the river.

If not the smallest museum in Britain (see page 141), the Ferry Hut is certainly one of the smallest. It was built about 100 years ago and measures just 9ft by 7ft, the sort of dimensions that put it in the shed class. After it lost its original purpose it took on a less illustrious role as a storage space. However, it was poorly maintained and may well have simply rotted away until it collapsed had it not been for one woman. Judi Hill, the chair of Alnmouth Parish Council, decided to take on the tenancy of the hut. She made a successful application for a grant and set about giving the hut a complete restoration.

She told the BBC in 2008: 'It had begun to look a bit derelict and I was worried it would become an eyesore and then be gone. So I gave it a clean-up, a builder came in to repair the walls and roof, and we gathered together as many photographs of the hut and its history as we could, which are displayed inside.'

And so the museum was founded. It's open every day and looked after by a local resident called Donald Blythe, whom you might also find sitting outside on a deckchair welcoming visitors. The exhibition he tends on the banks of the Aln is a wonderful mishmash of information about the ferry, assembled in the piecemeal fashion described by Judi Hill and all the more charming because of it. Framed photographs and newspaper cuttings adorn the hut's walls and there are little artefacts that tell the viewer something about the ferry or the local community it served.

This is not a place that overwhelms with a mass of facts and figures, and the only interactive element is the possibility of a chat with whatever locals may be around when you visit. However, the museum will give you an insight into the lost world of the Aln ferrymen. And after you've seen all you wish to see, you can feast your eyes on a view that they too would have recognised. It's a wide vista speckled with the same seabirds they knew – oystercatchers, redshanks, curlews and gulls – as they plied the waters of the Aln.

Useful information

Dinghy Park, Riverside Road, Alnmouth, Northumberland NE66 2SD
Usually open during daylight hours | Admission free;
donation appreciated

Getting there by public transport

From Alnmouth railway station, on the East Coast main line from London to Edinburgh, it's a 1½-mile walk to the museum. From the station approach turn left onto South View. Carry on over the roundabout onto the B1338. At Hipsburn Primary School you can catch the X18 bus (arrivabus.co.uk/north-east; 0344 800 4411) for a 3-minute bus ride into Alnmouth or simply carry on walking. Turn off Northumberland Street at Garden Terrace, which leads into Riverside Road. Look out for the museum on your right.

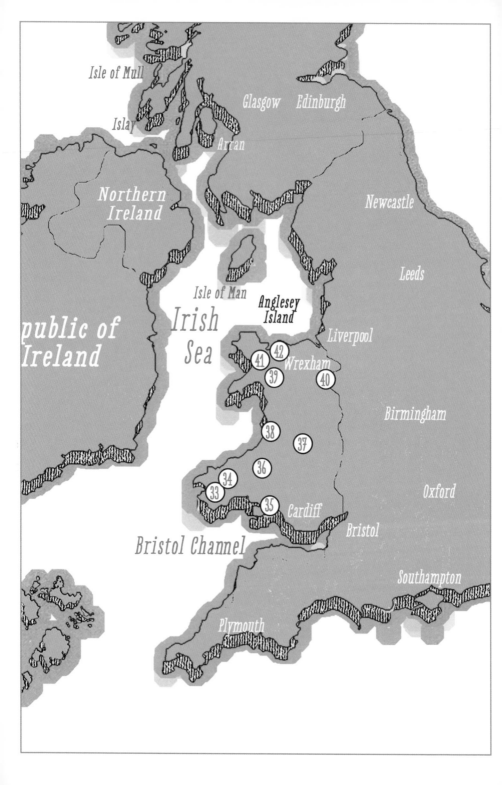

Wales

Tiny City
St Davids, Pembrokeshire

One of the most freeing things about being known as Britain's smallest city is that so little is expected of you. The first-time visitor to Glasgow, Birmingham, Cardiff or Bristol will assume that they will be entertained with élan; offered a cosmopolitan selection of locales in which to slake their thirst, sate their hunger and shop themselves bankrupt; and be presented with some tasty gobbets of culture that are simply not available in town and countryside. Even less populous cities such as Lincoln and Perth will bear some burden of expectation in this regard. But a city with a population of 1,841?

That's very much village territory and no one demands all that much of small communities nowadays when so many can no longer even muster up a post office; while the days of the folk of Albion Parva banding together to put on a production of the Ring cycle by Wagner in the village hall are gone the way of Capstan Full Strength cigarettes and ministerial integrity.

St Davids is an anomaly peculiar to Britain, of course. The kangaroo-shaped nation off the west coast of Continental Europe enjoys a singularly idiosyncratic relationship with the word 'city'. In other countries the term is reserved for centres of population that have grown too large to be called towns. As far as Britain is concerned it either has to do with the presence of a cathedral (or university in the case of Oxford and Cambridge) or harks back to the days when monarchs could bestow the title where'er they found it beneficial to do so. All that was necessary was to declare the largest church in the community a cathedral and – hey presto! – a city was founded. Henry VIII was particularly adept at the practice in the period after he dissolved the monasteries.

It has resulted in the absurd state of affairs in which little Ely in Cambridgeshire has been a city since 1109, while Manchester was only officially granted that status in 1853.

The wonderful thing about St Davids is that, although it obviously is small, it really repays all the effort expended in getting there. And unless you happen to live in the southwest corner of Wales, some effort will indeed be required, for the city has hidden itself towards the end of a coastal peninsula, many miles from anywhere. The only other niggle one might have with it is that somewhere over time St Davids' apostrophe has gone missing. Those rightly offended by this, however, can get around it by using the city's Welsh name, Tyddewi, which means 'David's house'.

The kangaroo-shaped nation off the west coast of continental Europe enjoys a singularly idiosyncratic relationship with the word 'city'

Surprisingly for a place so small, the city is not dominated by its really rather impressive cathedral (albeit one with a slightly stumpy tower). The reason for this is that it is set down in a dip on the outskirts of town next to another big draw – the extensive ruins of the Bishop's Palace. Mostly built by Bishop Henry de Gower in the first half of the 14th century, the palace rests on the site of a much-pillaged 6th-century monastery. The colossal edifice shows the medieval church at its most venal. There was clearly little expense spared and the banquets that were held there became legendary. The whole business about rich men, heaven, camels and eyes of needles seems to have been lost on the bishop. In the summer the ruined palace doubles as an open-air theatre, providing a memorable backdrop, and it's well worth timing your visit to coincide with a performance.

De Gower was also responsible for enlarging the cathedral next door, which has been a destination for

pilgrims for many hundreds of years. The village too merits a gander. It has a character all its own and is a place of colourful terraced houses, cosy little cafés and a very funky supermarket called CK's.

Embark on a coastal walk around the end of the peninsula that takes its name from the city and you'll soon encounter Porthclais, a picturesque little harbour complete with defunct lime kilns. The haven used to be the city's main port in the days when goods came in by sea. But before you reach it you'll pass by a holy well and the ruins of St Non's Chapel.

It is here, sometime around AD 500, that St Non is said to have given birth to a son, a boy who would go on to become the patron saint of Wales and lend his name to the smallest city in the land.

Useful information

St David's Cathedral: The Pebbles, St Davids, Pembrokeshire SA62 6RD Open daily 9am–5.30pm – for service times see website | Admission free (£5 donation suggested) | stdavidscathedral.org.uk | 01437 720202

Bishop's Palace: Open daily Mar–Jun and Sep–Oct 9.30am–5pm, Jul–Aug 9.30am–6pm, Nov–Feb Mon–Sat 10am–4pm, Sun 11am–4pm (last admission 30 minutes before closing), closed 24–26 Dec and 1 Jan | Adult £4, senior/student/children U16 £2.60, children U5 free, disabled and companion free, family (2+3) £11.90 cadw.gov.wales | 01437 720517

St Non's Chapel: On the clifftops due south of St Davids; follow signs from the information centre | Always open | Admission free | tinyurl.com/ydpjtkl

Getting there by public transport

Naturally, Britain's smallest city does not run to a railway station, so you'll have to hotfoot it to Haverfordwest on the line from Swansea to Milford Haven. From the station, a number 411 bus (richardsbros.co.uk; 01239 613756) will take you to St Davids in 45 minutes. Alternatively, take the train to Fishguard and Goodwick, almost the end of a line from Swansea, walk a few minutes to the Harbour Garage on The Parrog in Goodwick and pick up a number 413 bus (also Richards Bros) which will also get you to St Davids in around 45 minutes.

34

Tiny Castle
Wiston Castle, Pembrokeshire

Wales does love a castle. With over 600 of them to its name, the Celtic nation holds the world record for the greatest number of castles per square mile. Given the slowdown in building castles in recent centuries, it's a title it's unlikely ever to lose.

The strongholds come in all sizes, from hulking great monoliths such as Caerphilly, Caernarfon and Conwy to very early and much more modest fortresses. One of the choicest examples in this latter category can be found just to the north of the village of Wiston in the far southwest of Wales.

Wiston Castle sits on a hill in the midst of farmland with a ring of gorse covering its lower flanks. It's a classic motte-and-bailey castle. A 40ft-high mound rises above the surrounding terrain. Below it an impressive ditch encircles the motte, which is 60ft wide at the top and still bears the stone wall of its shell keep. The wooden buildings that would have been protected by this wall have long since gone, of course, but the wall itself has one very interesting feature: although it's circular inside, it's not circular outside – it has no fewer than 18 sides. It wouldn't be until later in the 13th century, when those returning from the Crusades brought back with them tales of fortresses with round towers, that castle designers began to favour the circular form. Round towers were better at deflecting cannon balls and other projectiles, and were less susceptible to toppling when undermined, and so proved very popular. Whenever it was that this wall was built, such qualities were of lesser value. Besides, an 18-sided wall must have looked very impressive,

and giving the impression of strength was very much part of one's defence against attack.

What makes Wiston Castle so special and where it differs from most of its contemporaries is that it was neither altered nor enlarged in step with the improvements in castle design that occurred throughout the Middle Ages. The vast majority of motte-and-bailey castles left in Britain today have been reduced to a motte (the sandcastle-shaped mound) and perhaps the odd ditch to show where the bailey (the outer wall) once was. Wiston, by contrast, is one of just half a dozen in Wales that have some remains of a stone keep. As one of the country's best preserved motte-and-bailey castles it offers up not only a faithful representation of what they were like but also gives visitors some insight into the lives of those who inhabited it.

The origins of the castle are somewhat uncertain, but according to Welsh-castles enthusiast Jeffrey L Thomas it was probably built, or at least started, by a Flemish colonist with the unlikely name of Wizo (or Gwys in Welsh). He was known to have settled in Pembrokeshire in the early 12th century, having corralled a band of fellow Flemish adventurers to take up the call of the Norman English King Henry I to colonise Celtic Wales.

Wizo had died by 1130 but not before he had selected the site of an Iron Age camp on which to build his castle. Such settlements were located on easily defendable land and often came with ready-made protective ditches so it is hardly surprising that Wizo's eye should have been caught by it when scoping out a locale for his castle. With a stockade thrown up as a bailey and a wooden fort on top, it would have sent a message to the dispossessed Welsh that there was a new power in the land. By 1112, Wizo is also credited with the construction of a church and the establishment of a small community.

The Welsh, undaunted, captured the motte-and-bailey fort in 1147 from Walter Fits Wizo ('fits', like the Irish 'fitz', simply meaning 'son of'). There are no existing documents that tell us the year Wiston castle was built, so the 1147 seizure by prince and poet Hywel ab Owain is the earliest event we know of to have taken place there. The castle must have fallen back into the hands of the Normans or their allies sometime later because the Welsh – this time led by one Hywel Sais ap Rhys – are recorded capturing the castle again in 1193, only to lose it again two years later to the Flemish colonists. Wiston Castle's real moment in the sun came in 1220 when it was seized by none other than Llywelyn the Great, Prince of Gwynedd. He was sweeping through South Wales, taking back territory that had been usurped by the English foe and their fellow travellers. Wiston's glory did not last long because Llewelyn ordered the castle to be destroyed, along with the settlement that had grown up alongside it.

However, it's possible that this did not signal the end of Wiston Castle. Henry III, still intent on securing Welsh land for his kingdom, commanded the Earl of Pembroke, William Marshal, to rebuild the castle. Marshal died in 1231, so any reconstruction on Henry's orders would presumably have taken place in the decade following Llywelyn the Great's destructive visit. Unfortunately, although there is archaeological evidence of two separate phases of rebuilding inside the keep, it's difficult to say whether the surviving wall is Marshal's work

Wiston Castle sits on a hill in the midst of farmland with a ring of gorse covering its lower flanks

or simply the remains that were left after 1220. For instance, the grand archway that pierces the wall on the southern side of the keep does appear to date from before the early 13th century. It would once have framed the wooden entrance gate and it's still possible to see the holes that held the drawbars, keeping it firmly shut against any intruders who had got past the large oval outer bailey and ditch.

The castle was still occupied in the 14th century – a family named Wogan had taken it over by then. A mansion house was built nearby and this somewhat overshadowed the castle, whose value as a fortified stronghold naturally waned as the centuries progressed.

It seems likely, however, that it did see one last flicker of action. During the Civil War, a small detachment of Royalists moved into Wiston and may have used the castle as a base. However, when the Parliamentarians moved through the area in force in 1644, the Cavaliers abandoned Wiston seemingly without a fight. By the 1700s, the motte had been relegated to the role of a quaint attraction on the estate of the manor house. Today, though very small in comparison with most Welsh castles, it remains an immaculate little piece of ancient Welsh history.

Useful information

Near Winston, Haverfordwest, Pembrokeshire SA62 4PN
Open daily 10am–4pm (last admission 3.30pm), closed 24–26 Dec and 1 Jan
Admission free
cadw.gov.wales | 0300 025 6000

Getting there by public transport

The 313 bus (Edwards Bros; 01437 890230) runs a few times a day from the bus station in Haverfordwest. This is a couple of minutes' walk from Haverfordwest railway station on the line between Carmarthen and Milford Haven. The bus takes just under half an hour to get to Wiston.

Tiny Cinema
Sol Cinema, near Swansea

While its claim to be the 'smallest cinema in the solar system' may not be strictly true, the Sol Cinema is certainly the smallest in Britain to be powered entirely by the sun. It's also one of the more peripatetic cinemas, since its screen, projector, red carpet and plush bench seating for eight are all fitted into a titchy vintage caravan. At just 9ft long and 7ft high, it can be towed almost anywhere.

The interior is a thing of kitsch beauty. The ceiling is painted to look like the sky, the walls are decked out in crimson and tan stripes and the seating is set out in two racked rows, the front benches complete with tassels. A low-energy LED video projector is set high on the back wall and there are surround-sound speakers dotted about to supply an aural experience that's rather more pleasurable than can be had at most conventional cinemas.

Although based on the Gower peninsula in South Wales, the Sol Cinema travels all over the country and occasionally further afield, often turning up at festivals. And like so much that is good in the world, the idea for it grew out of the fertile soil of social activism.

Back in the 1990s, documentary-maker Paul O'Connor spent a lot of his time training activists in the production of films. He was successful in getting the resultant shorts shown in village halls and community centres. These were the only places where they had a chance of being aired because there was little hope in getting the films broadcast on television or gracing the screens of normal cinemas. However, Paul and those he worked with longed to be able to put on films themselves

and thus reach a wider audience. The Sol Cinema provided the ideal solution.

In 2010 Paul asked his friend Jo Furlong and artists Ami and Beth Marsden if they could turn their hands to creating a cinema. A beaten-up twin-berth Bluebird Eurocamper built in 1972 was duly acquired and converted into the wonder it is today, mainly using recycled materials. Photovoltaic panels basking in the sun provide the power to show the films. It means that not only is the Sol Cinema a green machine, but off-grid as well, so it can put on a show pretty much anywhere.

Patrons pick up a ticket and some popcorn at the caravan window and saunter up a red carpet between two rope barriers, in the style of a VIP. Handing the ticket to a uniformed usherette (quite possibly the same one who gave it to them a few seconds beforehand), they can then settle in to watch a film or two. As a general rule, the Sol Cinema shows films that last between 60 seconds and 10 minutes – or the average length of time it takes to fall asleep in front of *Dances with Wolves* – so there's a good chance you'll still have some popcorn left when you leave. It's the future of cinema all right.

Useful information

Based on the Gower, near Swansea
Admission free | For dates and locations see thesolcinema.org; 07973 298359

Getting there by public transport

It's probably wise to find out where the caravan is first. If it's appearing somewhere at its home on the Gower, it can be reached by taking a train to Swansea and then hopping on one of the many buses that make the short journey onto the peninsula.

Tiny Town
Llanwrtyd Wells, Mid-Wales

The fact that Llanwrtyd Wells is the smallest town in Wales (predictably, it claims the 'smallest town in Britain' crown too) is not the most exceptional thing about the place by a long way. This 'blink and you've missed it' community by a couple of obscure valleys in the depths of Wales has transformed itself in recent years into a Mecca for those who wish to partake in bizarre, exhausting, mud-spattered and often ridiculous sports.

The World Bog Snorkelling Championships are held here every year, as is the Man versus Horse Marathon, while the World Alternative Games takes place every even year. If you've ever dreamed of being a world champion in something or other but have never found a sport that fits your personal skill set, it's worth coming along to Llanwrtyd Wells and trying your luck.

The town lies on the Afon Irfon, an unobtrusive river that picks its way through the southern Cambrian mountains en route to meet the Wye at Builth Wells. It's a most picturesque spot and, on those occasions when it stops raining, the 850 inhabitants enjoy fine views up into the hills. The town itself has a certain old-fashioned charm – large terraced houses line the more affluent streets, with smaller but still well-presented terraced houses on the less well-to-do thoroughfares.

If the sporting competitions succeed in making Llanwrtyd Wells famous, it will not be for the first time. As its suffix suggests, Llanwrtyd was once a spa town. This came about because the wonderfully

monikered Reverend Theophilus Evans happened to notice a frog in a well one day in 1732. The Reverend Evans was evidently something of a naturalist. While most folk wouldn't be able to tell the difference between a frog who was on absolutely tip-top form and one who was merely getting by, Evans was struck at just how healthy this particular specimen looked. He at once suspected that it was the water in the well that had caused the frog to be in such fine fettle and carried out investigations into the matter. He discovered that the water from the local spring was high in sulphur. One would have thought that the stench of sulphur would have given the game away sometime before this, rather than the sprightliness of a frog, but those were different times.

The Ffynnon Ddrewllyd ('stinking well') was soon drawing in the sick and the lame and those who knew that what was good for frogs must be good for people too. Llanwrtyd Wells, as it was soon dubbed, grew into a bustling and prosperous spa town as a result, which accounts for a lot of the large houses. It was already on the route of a popular stagecoach, but when the railway line arrived in 1867, health tourism boomed and the fame of the sulphurous health-giving waters of Llanwrtyd Wells spread far and wide.

It's a little sad, therefore, to see the moribund state of the 'stinking well' in the grounds of the Dol-y-Coed Hotel. The tourist trade dwindled and died in the 20th century as the vogue for taking the waters withered away. Still, at least the locals had the Cambrian Woollen Mill to fall back on. Built on land just outside the town, it was one of the last operating woollen mills in the country until its recent closure. At one point it employed 250 people in this sparsely populated area.

But it's not health or wool that Llanwrtyd Wells is known for nowadays, but outlandish sporting competitions. The World Alternative Games are basically the Olympics if the Olympics were fun. They're held biennially in August over 2½ weeks,

The World Bog Snorkelling Championships are held here every year, as is the Man versus Horse Marathon

mostly in and around Llanwrtyd Wells. They began in 2012 – inspired by London's successful bid to hold the Olympic and Paralympic Games that year. Llanwrtyd Wells had already started to gain a reputation by then for its curious sporting occasions and the organisers felt it might be amusing to put together a whole smorgasbord of arcane events in the space between the end of the Olympics and the beginning of the Paralympics that year. So compelling was the idea that it even gained the backing of the Welsh Assembly.

The Man versus Horse Marathon has been going since 1980. It was born out of a conversation in the Neuadd Arms Hotel about whether a horse or a human would be quicker over a long distance in the difficult terrain of the Cambrian mountains. A 22-mile course in the hills surrounding the town was agreed upon and the race was run, with a horse and rider winning easily.

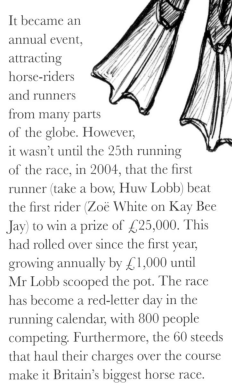

It became an annual event, attracting horse-riders and runners from many parts of the globe. However, it wasn't until the 25th running of the race, in 2004, that the first runner (take a bow, Huw Lobb) beat the first rider (Zoë White on Kay Bee Jay) to win a prize of £25,000. This had rolled over since the first year, growing annually by £1,000 until Mr Lobb scooped the pot. The race has become a red-letter day in the running calendar, with 800 people competing. Furthermore, the 60 steeds that haul their charges over the course make it Britain's biggest horse race.

Former singer and serial election also-ran Screaming Lord Sutch was the MC at many of the races and died a few days after performing this duty for the last time in 1999. A plaque commemorating his service to the race can be seen in the Neuadd Arms.

The World Bog Snorkelling Championships started in 1985 as a fundraising event to help build a new community centre in the town. Once again its origins can be traced back to the Neuadd Arms and, one suspects, a certain amount of alcohol. According to the history of the event recorded on the World Alternative Games website, a local woman named Iris Shrigley declared that 'the only thing she had in her garden was a bog'. This pronouncement was greeted by a cry of, 'Well, let's snorkel in it.' Instead, the event was held in a local bog in which a 60yd channel had been dug for the occasion.

Competitors had to swim two lengths while remaining below the surface of the murky waters, with only flippers, snorkel and goggles to aid them. It was a hit and has been held every year ever since.

These two events and 10 other oddities that were already up and running locally (such as the Mountain Bike Chariot Race and the Welsh Open Stone Skimming Championships – see page 251) were incorporated into the inaugural World Alternative Games along with a whole raft of other unorthodox ways of pitting competitors against each other. The first games in 2012 had 36 events (and 2,000 competitors) but this had mushroomed to 60 by 2014. Gold, silver and bronze medals are awarded to the first three athletes in each discipline but every entrant takes home a Corinthian medal to emphasise the fact that it really is the taking part that counts. Popular events include worm charming,

Russian egg roulette, husband dragging, finger jousting, the bicycle wrong way race and tractor pulling.

There are so many other activities going on all year round in Llanwrtyd Wells that it makes your head spin. The annual 10-day Mid Wales Beer Festival in November includes a 25-mile cycling challenge called the Real Ale Wobble; while the Mountain Bike Chariot Race takes place during January's Saturnalia Winter Warmer Real Ale Festival.

If this were not enough, the town is also an eisteddfod location and has a couple of pretty impressive pages from the history of Welsh music tucked away in its harp case. The oft-sung Welsh folk song *Sosban Fach* ('Little Saucepan') was written in the town. There's a plaque up on a building called Britannia House in Irfon Crescent to commemorate the fact.

But that is eclipsed by another song that has found fame beyond the Welsh borders. The next time you hear *Guide Me, O Thou Great Jehovah* (aka *Bread of Heaven*) sung with full-throated vigour before a rugby match at Cardiff Arms Park, think of Llanwrtyd Wells. The words to the hymn – set to the tune Cwm Rhondda by John Hughes – were written in the town (in Welsh) by Rev William Williams of Pantycelyn while on a three-year stint as a curate (working for notorious frog-spotter Rev Theophilus Evans, as it happens). One only hopes that Williams didn't get the inspiration for the lines 'Dere dy hunan/Dyna'r pryd y dof i maes' (lit. 'Do Thou grant/The occasion to escape') from where he was living at the time.

Useful information

You can get information about taking part in (or just watching) the World Alternative Games through their Facebook page. Applications for the triathlon, bog snorkelling and mountain bike chariot racing events must be made through www.green-events.co.uk

A useful round-up of what's going on in the town can be found at neuaddarmshotel.co.uk/events

Getting there by public transport

Despite its diminutive size, Llanwrtyd Wells has its own railway station. Llanwrtyd (the station comes without the 'Wells') is on the beautiful Heart of Wales line that runs from Swansea in South Wales to Shrewsbury in Shropshire (heart-of-wales.co.uk | 01554 820586

Tiny Church
St Mary's, Powys

On the slopes of a hill called Bryn Glas, tucked away in the trees and only accessible by a track, stands a little milk-white church with a dark slate roof. A simple nave with a squat tower at one end, St Mary's has been beautifully restored and lime-washed and is evidently cared for despite the infrequency of services held there nowadays (just four a year and all those in the summer months).

At first glance, there is nothing to suggest that it marks the place where an orgy of violence occurred – indeed, if anything, the church's calm lines and unfussy architecture appear to represent nothing but peace and tranquillity.

Although parts of St Mary's date as far back as the 13th century, it's by no means the first church on this site. The earliest record of a place of worship here is from 1198 and it's believed that there may have been a rustic chapel in this spot well before that. There was clearly a larger tower at some stage too, as is evidenced by the huge footings to the north of the

church. Close by you'll come across a holy well – a rubble-lined hole in the ground that once drew the sick and the halt from miles around seeking a cure from its miraculous waters.

St Mary's, also sometimes known as Our Lady of Pilleth, has not enjoyed the easiest of histories, as we shall see. One of its more recent brushes with catastrophe occurred on 3 March 1894 when the whole place went up in flames. Since it was not insured and the parish did not have the means to repair it, no restoration work was carried out immediately. When the weather allowed, services were held in the churchyard and it wasn't until

1910 that the fabric of the church was patched up well enough for it to be used again.

Despite its travails – and the fact that the interior's lime-washed rubble walls and flagstone floors are plain enough to set a Puritan's heart aflutter – there's plenty of interest to see inside. The communion table and two chairs were made in the 17th century. There's also a medieval chest and an oak frame for three bells, two of which vanished in the 19th century. The remaining one is really quite something – it was cast sometime around 1450 by one Richard le Beleyetere of Worcester and bears the inscription *Sancta Radegunda ora pro nobis*, an appeal to the now somewhat obscure St Radegunda to 'pray for us'. At one time you would also have been able to see a venerable sword, breastplate and spurs, but someone stole them in the 1990s and they've never been recovered.

St Mary's greatest claim to fame though is one it shares with another tiny St Mary's, far away in Yorkshire. The latter church looked on as the Battle of Towton – probably the bloodiest engagement ever fought on British soil – raged outside its walls on Palm Sunday 1461. Half a century earlier, St Mary's at Pilleth had a similar dubious honour when one of the most momentous battles in Welsh history was fought on its doorstep.

The Battle of Bryn Glas, sometimes known as the Battle of Pilleth, took place on 22 June 1402. It was an attempt by the English Earl of March, Sir Edmund Mortimer, to snuff out the nationalist rebellion led by one of the great Welsh heroes, Owain Glyndŵr. To be fair, Glyndŵr had been provoked into insurrection. In 1400 he had had land stolen from him and had been wrongly accused of treason by one Reginald Grey, a supporter of King Henry IV, a man who had controversially seized the throne from Richard II the year before. Prior to the battle, Mortimer (who

> *A simple nave with a squat tower at one end, St Mary's has been beautifully restored and lime-washed and is evidently cared for*

196

incidentally had a much better claim to the English throne than Henry) persuaded a force of Welsh archers to join his Herefordshire troops. There is a degree of uncertainty regarding the exact site of the battle but an extensive study carried out a few years ago concluded that the main focus of the fighting occurred on the slopes of Bryn Glas, probably to the east, south and west of the church, where the initial engagement of the opposing forces took place.

Glyndŵr held the summit of Bryn Glas ('green – or blue – hill') but, before Mortimer had arrived on the scene, he split his own army in two. He kept his archers with their longbows on the hill and hid the remainder of his troops in the narrow valley between Bryn Glas and Graig Hill immediately to the north. Mortimer already had a superior number of men under his command and the sight of a small body of archers on the hill must have given him further reason to believe that his enemy was weak and would be defeated easily. It would explain why he was happy to have his men march upwards into battle, which is rarely a wise tactic.

As Mortimer's men advanced, they came within range of Glyndŵr's archers, who had the advantage of firing their arrows downhill. Then the main force of Glyndŵr's army swept up out of the valley to launch a surprise attack on Mortimer's right flank. Seeing which way the wind was blowing (or it may be that they had always planned to do this), the Welsh archers in the English ranks suddenly swapped sides. The English were pushed back – possibly as far as the River Lugg, half a mile south of the church – and were then routed. Mortimer himself was captured. Shakespeare records a report of the battle right at the start of his surprise hit of summer 1597, *Henry IV (Part I)*:

> *A post from Wales loaden*
> *with heavy news;*
> *Whose worst was that the*
> *noble Mortimer,*
> *Leading the men of*
> *Herefordshire to fight*
> *Against the irregular and*
> *wild Glendower,*
> *Was by the rude hands of*
> *that Welshman taken,*
> *A thousand of his people butchered.*

Despite Shakespeare's confident and conveniently rounded estimate, it's actually impossible to gauge just how many soldiers died in the battle that day, though certainly more Englishmen than Welshmen breathed their last. Estimates of the English dead range from 200 to 1,100. A parcel of land has been planted with Wellingtonia trees to mark the place where an excavation revealed a large number of bones, which may well be the remains of those who fell here. A memorial to the dead on both sides can be viewed in the churchyard.

After their victory, the Welsh troops went on to sack and burn Leominster, an exploit that countless others have considered since but have lacked the necessary brio to carry out. The Welsh rebellion, far from being snuffed out, was burning brightly.

St Mary's did not survive the encounter unscathed either – Glyndŵr had it put to the torch. Thankfully, it was not completely destroyed and much of the peaceful church that sits on the hillside today is the work of hands that toiled to rebuild it after the fury of war had thundered away to other hillsides to bedevil other mortals.

Useful information

Pilleth, Knighton, Powys LD7 1NP
The church is always open and there are four services a year: 3pm on 4th Sun of Jun (Holy Communion to commemorate the Battle of Pilleth), Jul (Evening Prayer), Aug (Holy Communion) and Sep (Harvest Evening Prayer)

Getting there by public transport

Knighton railway station is on the Heart of Wales line from Shrewsbury to Swansea (heart-of-wales.co.uk; 01554 820586). From the bus station at Knighton you can take the T58 bus (Knighton Taxis; 01547 528165) or the number 41 (sargeantsbros.com; 01544 230481) to Whitton in Herefordshire. From there it's a 1¼-mile walk along the B4356 to Pilleth and its church, which is tucked behind Pilleth Court and accessible via a track.

38

Tiny Mine
Llywernog Mine, Ceredigion

Much is made of the various gold rushes that took place in the United States, Australia and elsewhere, which proved that sometimes that which glisters is the real thing. The discoveries of silver in Britain are somewhat less trumpeted, despite the fact that the precious metal has been mined since at least Roman times. However, the first cry that there was silver in them thar hills east of Aberystwyth went up much more recently – around 1742, when George II was on the throne.

The identities of the fortunate prospectors on that occasion have been lost but we do at least know what they did: they sank two shafts into the ground and joined them together with a passage that ran along the seam in which the silver deposit had been discovered. Over 250 years later, these first modest intrusions into the earth can still be seen.

As mines go, the one at Llywernog was always a very small-scale operation. It doesn't bear comparison with the dimensions of the average British coalmine and it's even

dwarfed by Cornwall's tin mines – the workings at Geevor, for example, extend for over 85 miles. However, it is an excellent example of *multum in parvo* (see page 131) – while the mine may be comparatively small, the pleasure one can derive from it is out of all proportion to its size.

That said, the mine was enlarged after that initial foray into the ground. Although it's often referred to as a silver mine, the lodes that were dug out contained a lead ore called argentiferous galena that is rich in the precious metal. Typically, such

ore comprises around 86% lead and 13% sulphur, with silver making up the last 1%, though sometimes it can be as high as 2–3%. In 1790, two adits (horizontal passages) were punched into the hillside. Hand drills, gunpowder, muscle and sweat were the order of the day and, in the case of one of the two tunnels, the toil proved worthwhile, striking a healthy seam of ore just 55ft below the surface.

Come the early years of the 19th century the lease for the mine was in the hands of a man named William Poole, who has lent his surname to the local name for the mine, Gwaith Poole ('Poole's work'). The Napoleonic Wars were in full spate and lead was in such demand that its price sky-rocketed. At its peak, 60 miners laboured to extract the ore, making Poole a very wealthy man. The lease for the mine changed hands many times as 'mine adventurers', some of them Cornish tin mine owners, came to try their luck at Llywernog. It meant that a vertical shaft that was tentatively begun in 1810 had reached a depth of 432ft by 1873, though all the while becoming less productive and more costly to pump out.

The following year, a pump with a 50ft-diameter waterwheel was erected at the mine to cope with the water that was filling the ever-deepening shaft. Unfortunately, just a few years later, enormous lead deposits were discovered in the US and Australia, which led to a slump in the price of the commodity and the wheel at Llywernog and several other Welsh lead mines stopped turning. After a brief attempt in the early 1900s to reactivate the mine in the search for zinc ore, Llywernog was finally abandoned.

That might have been the end of the story had it not been for the Harvey family who bought the site in 1973. The mine buildings – most of which dated from the 19th century – were extremely dilapidated but at least they still existed, which was no longer the case at the three other mines in this western part of the Cambrian mountains. The Harveys renovated them, made the tunnels safe, gathered the machinery together so that it could be exhibited and opened the mine as a museum the following year. More recently, in 2012, the museum was given a complete overhaul, turning it into a much more interactive attraction called the Silver Mountain Experience. Visitors can now go on three different guided tours including the 45-minute Miners' Trail which takes in the old mine offices before heading underground, entering by one of the adits that was driven into the hill back in 1790, and ending up at an exhibition of mining paraphernalia. There's also something called Time Lab, which is a live action show in which actors play out the history of the mine in dramatic form. Black Chasm is a tour that takes visitors underground on a spine-chilling journey into the darker side of Welsh myths and legends. Meanwhile, for young children, there's A Dragon's Tale, in which the little mites are taken on a hunt for a shy dragon by the name of Grotty.

If that were not entertainment enough, you can also try your hand at

> Many men lost their lives in accidents at Llywernog over the years and their restless souls are said to maunder about the mine workings

panning for fool's gold (which is not, apparently, meant as a puckish satire of contemporary mores).

There is another side to this tiny mine that cannot be ignored. Llywernog happens to rank very high on the list of the most haunted places in Wales. Accordingly, organised paranormal investigations take place here at night, led by a team of experts in such matters and open to (paying) members of the public.

Many men perished in accidents at Llywernog over the years and their restless souls are said to maunder about the mine workings and the surrounding woods. After the session ends at 2am, you can even pitch a tent in the grounds and spend the night among the wraiths and strays.

Useful information

The Silver Mountain Experience, Llywernog, Ponterwyd, Aberystwyth, Ceredigion SY23 3AB

Open daily Apr–early Nov 10am–4pm or 10am–5pm (last admission an hour before closing).There are also special evening and Christmas events and a period in autumn when only groups are allowed (checking the website before you go is strongly advised) | Adult £12.95, senior/student £11.50, children (4–15) £9.95, children U4 free (advance tickets can be purchased online for a 10% discount) – ticket prices include all surface attractions plus one of the three accompanied tours (Black Chasm, A Dragon's Tale or The Miners' Trail) | Extra tours: adult £4, senior/student £3.50, children £3 silvermountainexperience.co.uk | 01970 890620

See website for details of the paranormal investigations.

Getting there by public transport

From Aberystwyth railway station, a terminus on the line from Shrewsbury, it's a 2-minute walk to the bus station where you can pick up the number 525 bus (midwalestravel.co.uk; 01970 828288) which stops right outside the Silver Mountain Experience.

39

Tiny Station
Plas Halt, Gwynedd

When it comes to small, secretive railway stations that appear to be inhabiting a dream, you'd be hard pressed to top Plas Halt. Buried in a wood on a mountainside in North Wales, with a single short and very low platform and a single short and very basic stone shelter, its primitive minimalism is wonderful to behold.

It's the sort of place where one could sit tranquilly for hours and simply ponder the nature of existence, perhaps with a volume of Simone de Beauvoir perched artlessly on a knee and a small hip flask of absinthe nestling comfortably in a pocket.

The fact that Plas Halt is served exclusively by trains hauled behind brave little steam locomotives merely adds to the sense that this is a station we all have a collective idea about, rather than one that actually exists. It's a request stop too, so not every train will necessarily halt here. A station called Tan-y-Bwlch, a few twists and turns further up the line, is the most important intermediate

stop on the Ffestiniog Railway and so if any busyness is to occur it occurs there, with very few passengers disturbing the peace at Plas Halt. Meanwhile, the next station on the way down the line is distant Penrhyn, a station near the coast that serves the village of Penrhyndeudraeth.

It takes roughly half an hour of huffing and puffing to get passengers from sea level at Porthmadog to Plas Halt, 375ft up into Snowdonia. The line here was built in 1836 to facilitate the transport of dressed slate from the mines further up at Blaenau Ffestiniog down to the awaiting ships at Porthmadog that would set sail around the globe. Before then, the slate had to be taken by pack mule down the mountain to the River Dwyryd and then conveyed in boats before being loaded into ships, all of which was very time consuming. The loaded wagons were rolled down the 13½-mile railway and hauled back up by horses. It was only in the early 1870s that an engineer called Robert Fairlie came up with a powerful enough steam locomotive to pull wagons up the steep inclines on such narrow gauge tracks (the rails are just 23½ inches apart).

However, it wasn't until 1963 that a station was opened at Plas Halt ('hall halt' in Welsh). Such was the simplicity of the original stop that the whole thing was constructed in an evening and a morning. Its purpose was to allow holidaymakers easy access to chalets planned at Plas Tan y Bwlch ('hall beneath the pass'), the house on the 100-acre estate that lends the station its name and which belonged to the quarry-owning Oakeley family until 1961. The Oakeleys used to have their own private station nearby but that has since been abandoned.

There's a private station that's still in use just a little further up the mountain at Coed-y-Bleiddiau. It serves a Victorian cottage that is half a mile from the nearest road

up an intimidatingly steep footpath. It seems the perfect place for a spy to hang out, and indeed it was. The residence was used as a holiday home by a group of families, including that of the Cambridge spy ring's 'Third Man', Kim Philby.

Nowadays, passengers who have the good sense to alight at Plas Halt fall into three parties. Some come to attend residential courses at the Snowdonia National Park Authority's Environmental Studies Centre which opened in Plas Tan y Bwlch in 1975. Others are heading for that same centre's extensive gardens, which are open to the public and whose *pièce de résistance* is a 120-year-old rhododendron tunnel. Visitors can sometimes look around the house as well (and there's a tearoom too, of course). The remainder are drawn here by the lure of the fine walking in these parts and the spectacular views down towards the sea or into the Vale of Ffestiniog. The Mawddach-Ardudwy Trail runs close by. This makes it possible to take the train up to the halt, spend some time contemplating life/Simone de Beauvoir/the rank undrinkability of absinthe under the roof of the station's stone shelter (built by volunteers in 1989), and then walk back down to the coast one of two ways. In one direction the path shadows the railway line all the way into Porthmadog. In the other, it descends into the Vale of Ffestiniog on its way to The Grapes at Maentwrog, the oldest coaching inn in Wales, before arriving at Llandecwyn station on the main Cambrian Coast line.

However, for lovers of scenes in which the beauty of a simple structure complements the natural beauty around it, the station makes for a destination in and of itself.

Useful information

Ffestiniog Railway: The scheduling is complicated and you should consult the website before planning a trip. As a guide, there are several trains daily during the summer and fewer trains on fewer days in other months | There are many different ticketing options, but a third-class 'half-way return' to Plas Halt from either Porthmadog or Blaenau Ffestiniog should cost around £14–£16 (first class roughly an extra £7) | Single tickets for the whole line, breaking the journey at Plas Halt, are available on request | There are also combined tickets covering the railway journey and entrance to the gardens at Plas Tan y Bwlch| festrail.co.uk | 01766 516024
NB Plas Halt is a request stop, so do make sure that the train will stop here before embarking.

Plas Tan y Bwlch Gardens: Open daily all year 10am–5pm; house opening hours vary – call ahead for details | Tearoom open Easter–Oct 11am–4pm Adult £4, children £2 | snowdonia.gov.wales/study-centre | 01766 772600

NB It's also possible to stay at the house on a B&B or DB&B basis – see website for details.

Getting there by public transport

For such an out-of-the-way place, Plas Halt is really quite easy to get to by public transport. Take a train to Porthmadog on the Cambrian Coast line that runs between Machynlleth and Pwllheli (walesonrails.com), and then change to the Ffestiniog Railway (details above) for the climb up to Plas Halt. Alternatively, get yourself to Blaenau Ffestiniog station, the terminus of the Conwy Valley line (conwyvalleyrailway.co.uk), and take a Ffestiniog Railway train down to Plas Halt. Either option is a joy.

Tiny Long-Distance Footpath
Maelor Way/Llwybr Maelor, Northeast Wales

When the Wales Coast Path opened for custom in 2012, it became the longest waymarked footpath in Britain. Coming in at a staggering 870 miles, it trounced the previous record held by the South West Coast Path with its more than respectable 630 miles. Scotland's longest footpath, the Cape Wrath Trail, measures over 200 miles but is a stroll in the park by comparison. Should you wish to combine the Wales Coast Path with the Offa's Dyke Path in a bid to walk more or less around the whole of Wales, you're in for a hike of around 1,000 miles.

Though no doubt very enjoyable, not everyone can devote that amount of time to circumperambulating the Principality. That's why it's so refreshing to find that not all of Britain's waymarked long-distance footpaths are actually all that long. At 24 miles, the Maelor Way is one of the shortest and could potentially be walked in a day as a challenge, especially since the ascents along its length total just 1,835ft. However, in order to savour the delights of the route, it's preferable to take a couple of days over it. It thus makes for a perfect weekend jaunt.

The Maelor Way owes its existence largely to a desire to get some more important paths to link up, a job it does very effectively. Taking its name from the ancient frontier region which now lies entirely within the Wrexham County Borough, the trail connects the Offa's Dyke Path in the west to four major routes in the east: the Sandstone Trail, Marches Way,

Shropshire Way and South Cheshire Way. On account of the complexities of the Welsh/English border in these parts, although the Maelor Way runs more or less east–west, it somehow manages to start and finish in Shropshire while spending the vast majority of its time either in Wales or striding along the border. On the way it utilises public footpaths, bridleways, minor roads and the towpath of the Llangollen Canal.

It's an exceptionally rural path. Although it visits the villages of Hanmer, Penley and Overton-on-Dee, and passes close to the little town of Chirk, it prefers to roam across farmland, linger in woods, or shadow the Rivers Dee and Ceiriog. Seekers after tranquillity and country air are definitely well catered for.

At Overton, the Maelor Way pays homage to one of the Seven Wonders of Wales:

Pistyll Rhaeadr and Wrexham steeple,
Snowdon's mountain without its
people,
Overton yew trees, St Winefride's
wells,
Llangollen bridge and Gresford bells

These four lines of doggerel were penned by an anonymous English traveller, probably in the late 18th century. They supposedly captured the essence of all that was best in Wales (or Mid- and North Wales to be more precise) at the time.

Overton's yews are still there: 23 of them stand guard around St Mary's church. Yews can be impressively long-lived and the most venerable among these are thought to have been planted in medieval times.

After Overton, the Maelor Way piggybacks the Wat's Dyke Way for a long stretch. While Offa's Dyke is almost universally known and celebrated, Wat's Dyke is practically unheard of outside its native district despite being one of the largest archaeological monuments in Britain.

In its heyday it was over 6ft high with a 6ft ditch, and it stretched for over 40 miles from near Maesbury in Shropshire to the Dee Estuary. It provided a *cordon sanitaire* between the Saxon kingdom of Mercia to the east and the territory of the Celts to the west. The River Severn helpfully provided a border southwards to the Bristol Channel. No one is exactly sure who built the dyke, when they built it, or who 'Wat' might have been (or if there even *was* a Wat – the name could simply derive from the Anglo-Saxon word for 'wet' or 'rough').

Not long after passing south of Chirk, the Maelor Way joins up with

the Offa's Dyke Path and its work is done.

Assuming you have no plans to tackle Offa's Dyke, it's definitely worth heading back east into Chirk to visit the mightily impressive fortress. And while you're there you can casually mention to anyone who'll listen that you've just come from walking a long-distance footpath from end to end. You don't have to go into details about precisely which one it was.

Useful information

The trail runs west from Grindley Brook (OS map reference SJ 521 432) to a point (SJ 264 374) between the hamlets of Bronygarth and Castle Mill. The Guide to the Maelor Way by Gordon Emery is a useful book to acquire before going. It's full of interesting and helpful information about the walk and contains detailed maps of the route. It's available for £1 from the Tourist Information Centre at Lambpit Street, Wrexham LL11 1AR
Open Mon–Fri 10am–4pm | 01978 292015

Getting there by public transport

To arrive at the eastern end of the trail, find your way to Whitchurch railway station on the Welsh Marches line twixt Newport and Crewe. From there walk the short distance to the Smithfield Shopping Centre from where a number 41 bus (Aintree Coachlines; 01513 271078) will whisk you along the A41 to Grindley Brook in a lightning-fast 5 minutes. If you're starting at the western end of the Maelor Way, head for the Chester to Shrewsbury line, and specifically Chirk/Y Waun railway station. Just outside you can hop on the number 64 bus (easycoach.co.uk – yet another tentacle of the Easy empire, though at the time of going to press the website still wasn't up and running) to Castle Mill, after which it's a matter of a few minutes' walk south to the start/end of the Maelor Way.

41

Tiny River
Afon y Bala, Gwynedd

Some rivers were born to greatness, some rivers have greatness thrust upon them, and some – like Afon y Bala – never seek it in the first place. The shortest river with a name in the whole of Britain does not begin at some spring up in the mountains, nor does it end by flowing out to sea. Rather it spends its entire brief life ferrying water from one lake, Llyn Peris, to another, Llyn Padarn.

To carry out this task it covers just 440yd but somehow manages to get more into that short space than many rivers manage in a county's worth of meanderings.

The mountains of Snowdonia form one of Britain's most glorious landscapes. A jumble of snaggle-toothed alps create both an arresting prospect and a formidable obstacle to anyone attempting to cross the northwest corner of Wales. However, there are a few gaps in the defences of this seemingly implacable mountain range, the most famous of them being the Llanberis Pass. Between them, Llyn Peris and Llyn Padarn have

helped to create this narrow corridor through the peaks, right under the glare of Snowdon (or Yr Wyddfa in Welsh), the highest mountain in Wales. This is the charming and much-loved strait that the Afon y Bala ('river [that is] an outlet of a lake') calls home. It's a curious thing that a pass so well known contains a river whose merits go almost entirely unsung.

The ruins of an ancient fortress towards the western end of Llyn Peris overlook the place where the Afon y Bala comes into being. Dolbadarn Castle was probably thrown up around 1230 by no less a man than

Llywelyn ap Iorwerth, or Llywelyn the Great as he is usually known to English speakers. It's an outstanding example of a castle constructed by native Celts, as opposed to the string of larger ones built half a century later by the Norman English invader Edward I. Dolbadarn sits on a little knoll, guarding this strategically important pass through the mountains. It's a shame that only the keep has survived the ravages of time more or less intact, but what a fine keep it is. Nearly 50ft high, the round stone tower lords it over the lake. With the Snowdonian mountains acting as a backdrop, it adds a splash of human drama to the scene.

It's a curious thing that a pass so well known contains a river whose merits go almost entirely unsung

Llywelyn the Great's grandson was Llywelyn ap Gruffydd and became known as Llywelyn the Last. The leader of the Welsh resistance was eventually defeated by Edward I and killed near Builth in 1282. His brother Dafydd ap Gruffydd took up the cudgels but the following year his forces were pushed south from the coast into Snowdonia. He made Dolbadarn his headquarters and administrative offices but before the year was out he had been captured and executed. The castle too fell into the hands of Edward's army. The king began to build his infamous chain of castles along the Welsh coast, with Caernarfon – 6 or 7 miles away to the northwest – as the new centre of government. Dolbadarn became surplus to requirements and its days as a military stronghold were over. The castle was relegated to the status of a manor house but at some unknown point it was abandoned and left to moulder.

Unlike humans, stone buildings often grow more beautiful when they are left to decay and the picturesque ruins inspired J M W Turner to capture them in oils in 1800. The painting can be seen today at the National Library of Wales in Aberystwyth.

Llyn Peris, the lake that gives birth to the Afon y Bala, is just over a mile long and takes its name from St Peris, the patron saint of drizzle. The glacial lake cradled by the Elidir

Fawr mountain on one side and the Derlwyn and Clogwyn Mawr hills on the other is best known, if known at all, for being the home of the Dinorwig power station. The plant generates electricity at times of peak demand by letting water flow down into the lake from Marchlyn Mawr, a reservoir up above. The water is then pumped back up using electricity when demand is low.

Almost as soon as the Afon y Bala has left Llyn Padarn it dives for cover under a road bridge. This used to carry traffic to the Dinorwig slate quarry from Llanberis, a large village a little separated from the river's left bank by the utilitarian charm of a sewage works. The latter is carved out of ground that climbs steeply from the right bank. The Afon Hwch – the Afon y Bala's only tributary – slides in from the south, bringing water it has collected from the slopes behind Llyn Peris. At least it's probably the Afon Hwch. The river joins forces with the larger Afon Arddu higher up and in some quarters it's reckoned that the mightier of the two waterways should be given the honour of retaining its name all the way down to the Afon y Bala. No matter, 'Hwch' is the name on a bridge that crosses the river near its end, which is evidence that would swing most juries.

Shortly afterwards (though, to be honest, nothing is longer than 'shortly' on the Afon y Bala), two bridges cross the river at almost the same point. The second is a small footbridge that carries walkers over from Llanberis towards Snowdonia's far northern hills. The first conveys a narrow-gauge railway line.

Not to be confused with the Snowdon Mountain Railway which heads out of Llanberis to take on the eponymous 3,560ft summit, the Llanberis Lake Railway is a much less giddy affair. After crossing the Afon y Bala, it strikes out along the northern shore of Llyn Padarn, following the route of the Padarn Railway, the line that was opened there in the 1820s. This was used to convey slate from the Dinorwig quarry (sometimes spelled Dinorwic) 7 miles to Port Dinorwic on the Menai Strait. However, when the Llanberis Lake Railway gets close to the far tip of the lake, a couple of miles away, it comes to a halt, because less is more. The railway's locomotives are very much in the Thomas the Tank Engine style. They used to belong to the Dinorwig quarry and would have ended up in a scrapyard had they not been restored and put to work on this shorter version of the old slate line. Now they live out their days hauling little lime green carriages full of happy tourists who gaze up at Snowdon and find some sort of evanescent fulfilment therein.

The main station on the line is called Gilfach Ddu and is perched on the north bank of the Afon y Bala. It's just where the river makes a slight dogleg to the left, the sole change of course along its length.

The station was named after the Victorian quarry workshops which once resounded to the clatter and ring of hammer on metal and the low menacing growl of the forge but which now house the National Slate Museum. Dinorwig quarry closed in 1969 and the museum recreates what it was like to work there as well as telling what the blurb assures visitors is 'the gripping story of slate'. Curiously, the whole place stands on what used to be the lake. So much spoil from the quarry was unceremoniously dumped into Llyn Padarn that new land was formed. Not only did this give the quarry owners some much-needed level ground on the north side of the water, but it also nearly doubled the length of the Afon y Bala.

But even so, in a few more blinks of an eye, the river has swept past the museum and entered the lake. Llyn Padarn, into which the Afon y Bala makes its far from headlong descent, is a 2-mile long stretch of water. It was formed long ago by the actions of a local glacier. As was the case with Llyn Peris, the numerous rocks shifted by the glacier not only gouged out the dip in which the lake formed but dammed it too, allowing the hollow to fill up with water. Llyn Padarn may only reach a maximum depth of 94ft, which is shallow when compared with Scottish lochs (see page 289), but combined with its 240-acre surface area it ranks as one of the largest lakes in Wales. Its waters will eventually flow out to sea via the Afon Seiont, their progress superintended by Edward's mighty castle at Caernarfon. But the Afon y Bala cares nothing about that – its job is done as soon as it releases its icy fresh waters into the lake.

Useful information

National Slate Museum: Open daily Easter–Oct 10am–5pm Nov–Easter daily except Sat 10am–4pm | Admission free | museum.wales/slate | 0300 111 2333

Llanberis Lake Railway: Check the website for the days on which the railway operates and the fluctuating timetable | Adult return from Gilfach Ddu £9, children £4.50, concessions for families, dog £1 lake-railway.co.uk | 01286 870549

Dolbadarn Castle: Open daily all year except 24–26 Dec and 1 Jan 10am–4pm (last admission 30 min before closing) | Admission free cadw.gov.wales; 0300 025 6000

Getting there by public transport

From Bangor, which is on the North Wales Coast line between Crewe and Holyhead, board the 85 bus (expressmotors.co.uk; 01286 881108) to Llanberis and take the footpath from the junction of Goodman Street and the A4086 to the western end of the river.

42

Tiny House
Quay House, Conwy

The Tiny House Movement is a thing nowadays. Its current incarnation got going in the United States in the 1990s, inspired in part by *Walden*, a book by Henry David Thoreau published in 1854 in which the author records his experiences of living for two years, two months and two days in a self-built cabin in the woods. The passion for bijou residences crossed the Atlantic to Britain as people became interested in seeking a simpler, cheaper, more pared-down way of living.

There's now a sizeable corner of cyberspace in which enthusiasts pore over innovative ideas for getting the most out of the meagre square footage of floorspace in one's cabin/trailer/micro-cottage/yurt/repurposed shipping container etc. It's really quite addictive and comes with its own make-do-and-mend, up-cycling, generally eco-friendly, living-a-little-bit-closer-to-nature, getting-out-of-the-rat-race philosophy.

However, no matter how ingenious, novel and well-crafted a new tiny house might be, it's never going to beat an old one around which you can get a tour from a Welsh woman in traditional Welsh costume – black funnel hat, red cape and all. By a strange coincidence, that's exactly what you get at Conwy's Quay House, better known by its other name 'The Smallest House in Great Britain'.

And there's no denying that it really is small. The owners like to give the measurements in inches to emphasise just *how* small it is: 72in

wide, 122in high and 120in deep. That's 6ft x 10ft 2in x 10ft, which works out at 610 cubic feet – roughly the equivalent of six of the classic K2 telephone boxes squidged together. And since the house is always painted bright red, it makes it easy to imagine it being half a dozen telephone boxes' worth of space.

Quay House is a minor tourist attraction nowadays but for hundreds of years it was a bona fide residence, albeit a cramped one. Given the lack of room there is in which to manoeuvre, each 5-minute tour is restricted to a maximum of two or three visitors, which does have the advantage of keeping it nice and personal. In that short time you'll hear a necessarily potted history of the house. It was built sometime in the 16th century as a sort of afterthought. There were two properties of more conventional dimensions with a gap in between them and someone thought to fill it with a house, despite the fact that there was patently not enough space for a proper one.

Thrillingly, the back wall is a section of one of the towers dotted around Conwy's ancient town walls. The other two walls were provided by the houses on either side, leaving the builder with the simple job of throwing up a front wall with two holes for windows and one for a very low door, then slapping a sloping roof on top. Looking at it today one wouldn't guess that this was what had happened. There is no house to the left, which gives the impression that Quay House is an end-of-terrace affair. The reason for this is that in 1900 Quay House and the houses to the left of it were all condemned as unfit for human habitation. While the other houses were summarily demolished, Quay House was saved for the nation specifically because it was so singularly small and it was felt (rightly, as it turned out) that it would make an interesting tourist attraction.

As the name Quay House suggests, the building is right on Conwy's very attractive harbourside, so it's unsurprising that its final resident was a fisherman. What is surprising is that he was reputedly 6ft 3in tall, which is about 2ft more than the optimum height for anyone attempting to live there. His name was Robert Jones and he was obliged to find other accommodation when the order condemning the houses was made.

It's difficult to believe it can have been much of a wrench to leave because, aside from the fact that his home didn't meet basic decent living conditions (even those pertaining to late Victorian times), he wouldn't have been able to stand up straight in either of his rooms.

This will become only too apparent should you visit. The ground floor is what we might call the lounge if we were being generous. As with the bedroom above, it has been kept in the style that its 19th-century occupants would have recognised. In the uneven back wall there's an open fireplace which would have taken coal. Naturally, there wouldn't have been a great deal of room to store the coal, but the advantage of having to heat such a small space is that it wouldn't have taken much fuel to do so. On each side of the fire is a minute range that would have been just about big enough to cook on if you didn't attempt anything too fancy. Candlesticks line the mantelpiece (there was no lighting installed) and a few pieces of crockery are kept in a compact glass-fronted cabinet. A little bench seat and a small table make up the remainder of the fixtures and fittings. Most of the walls and the mighty oak beams that cross the

Quay House is a minor tourist attraction nowadays but for hundreds of years it was a bona fide residence

ceiling are painted black, adding to the claustrophobic atmosphere. When there was a fire in the grate it must have been fuggy indeed.

It's no longer possible to enter the bedroom upstairs because it has become structurally unsound. However, visitors are allowed to climb the ladder to look into it. What they'll see is another very small fireplace, a single bed with an iron bedstead and a niche cut into the wall behind it to provide shelves for a few possessions. There's no bathroom, a fact about which it's probably best to draw a veil, but there is at least a water tap in what passes for a stairwell.

Prior to Robert Jones' tenancy, the house is known to have been rented by couples, which must have proved quite an extreme test of their relationship.

In 1900, the house's owner lived next door (to the right) at 11 Lower Gate Street. He too was called Robert Jones. He is said to have been rather unwillingly dragged around Britain by the editor of the *North Wales Weekly News* in order to verify that his was indeed the smallest house in Britain. Many years later, Guinness World Records came to the same conclusion.

It's gratifying to note that Quay House and no. 11 have both been kept in the Jones family, having been passed down the distaff side, so a connection to its last (slum) landlord has been maintained. After your five minutes of fun, do find the time to amble along the walkways on top of Conwy's venerable town walls. As befits a place in possession of such a tiny house, it's one of the smallest walled towns in Britain and a World Heritage Site.

The castle's not bad either, though rather on the large side for those seeking out the smaller pleasures Britain has to offer.

Useful information

10 Lower Gate Street, Conwy LL32 8BE
Open daily Mar–Nov 10am–6pm during school holidays and 10am–4pm at other times | Adult £1, children U17 50p
thesmallesthouse.co.uk | 01492 573965

NB May close early in bad weather or stay open later in the event of there being a long queue.

Getting there by public transport

Conwy railway station is a request stop on the North Wales Coast line between Crewe and Holyhead so you'll have to ask the guard to have the train stop there. It's a very easy walk to the house from the station. Cross Rose Hill Street and saunter down the High Street to the harbour. Turn left and Quay House is a short distance along on your left.

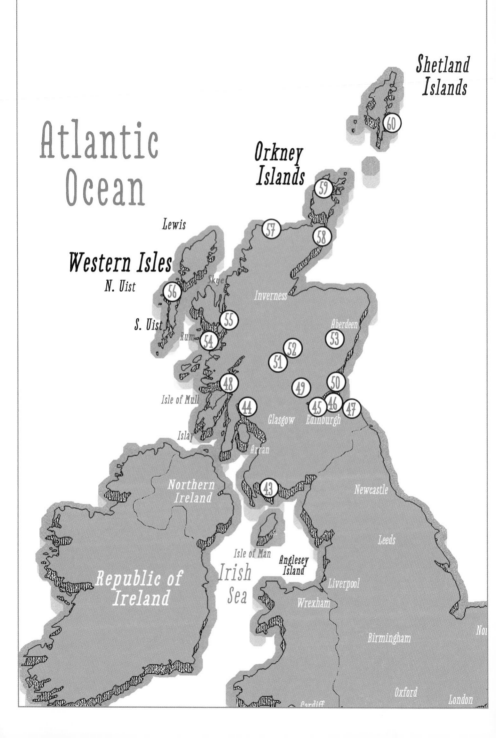

Atlantic
Ocean

Shetland
Islands

60

Orkney
Islands

59

57

58

Lewis

Western Isles

N. Uist

56

Skye

Inverness

S. Uist

55

Aberdeen

Rum

54

53

52

51

48

49

50

Isle of Mull

44

45 46

47

Glasgow

Edinburgh

Islay

Arran

Northern
Ireland

43

Newcastle

Isle of Man

Anglesey
Island

Leeds

Republic of
Ireland

Irish
Sea

Liverpool

Wrexham

Birmingham

Nor

Cardiff

Oxford

London

~ Scotland ~

Tiny Theatre
The Swallow Theatre, Dumfries and Galloway

Lost in pasture on a peninsula of Dumfries and Galloway that is seldom troubled even by those doughty tourists who make it as far as the literary hub of Wigtown, there is a converted byre. Unusually, that byre was not converted from housing cows to housing holidaymakers but became a theatre, the smallest one in Scotland. The story behind its creation is rather heart-warming and shows just what can be achieved with a little application.

The Swallow Theatre has just 50 seats. The website warns that these are 'quite comfortable but some people like to bring a cushion'. Even this is still something of a step up though because there was a time in the theatre's early days when audience members were asked to bring along their own chairs. It's all part and parcel of the nature of the place – 'the play's the thing' here (or at least 'the performance is the thing' – and had Shakespeare thought to write that instead, the phrase would enjoy a far wider application today

than it does) and if the audience has to muck in a little from time to time then that's part of the community spirit the theatre wishes to engender.

Moss Park is a small group of stone outbuildings clustered around a farmhouse. From the outside, the byre still has the look of a cowshed: whitewashed walls, a blue door and the sort of old-school industrial roofing still seen on barns from Shetland to the Isles of Scilly. Only a rather classy sign on the wall advertises the fact that this is now a theatre. Inside, there's a smallish

stage, as might be imagined, and a fully retractable raked seating area, which comes as more of a surprise. A foyer-cum-box-office-cum-bar meets all ticketing and refreshment needs, and there's a small garden with a pond to which theatre-goers are invited to take a picnic. So if you've always wanted to take a hamper along to Glyndebourne but find the seat prices there a little beyond your purse, the Swallow makes for a charming and inexpensive alternative.

The theatre now runs to its own office. There's also accommodation for visiting performers and groups needing somewhere to use as a bolthole to rehearse. It's certainly come a long way from the days when the swallows that nest in the outbuildings (and after whom the theatre is named) used to enliven performances in the barn by casually swooping in to feed their young.

It was a dream shared by two people that brought the Swallow Theatre into existence. Jill and David Sumner bought Moss Park in 1990 and began to put on play readings for a few friends and acquaintances. Gradually, these became more popular – the audience expanding from just three to 30 – and so in 1995 the couple took the decision to convert their cowshed into a space

> There was a time in the theatre's early days when audience members were asked to bring along their own chairs

that could be used not only for theatrical performances but also for musicians, poets and visual artists.

Planning permission was sought and obtained and the theatre's first five shows were staged the following summer while the extensive building work was in full flow. In the arts world, necessity very often becomes the mother of invention, and in one production a pile of sand ready for use in the renovation was craftily incorporated into the set. The first play to be staged was fresh from Jill Sumner's own pen – a work entitled *The Last Post* which dealt with events around the Battle of the Somme.

In the following couple of years, as audiences increased, the requests for theatre-goers to bring along their own seats were made. A lottery grant and a 'Sponsor a Seat' appeal eventually put an end to this rather endearing practice. Nowadays, the selection of events you can see in the theatre's own seats ranges from plays (old and brand new) and poetry recitals to folk, jazz and classical concerts and charity events. The venue also has its own supporting charity, the Swallow Theatre Association, whose support helps bring in professional productions that would not otherwise make it to such out-of-the-way spots as this.

Sadly, Jill Sumner died in 2001, just five years after the theatre opened in earnest. David remained here until 2016, when new owners took over, vowing to carry on staging top-quality professional events and celebrating the theatre's 20th season by staging a new adaptation of *The Last Post*.

But this is not just a place to see others perform. If you fancy yourself as an aspiring thespian, or just want to dip your toe in the water, you can attend one of the theatre's monthly play readings. Everyone can have a go and plays include classics such as J B Priestley's *An Inspector Calls*. Tea and coffee provided. And chair too.

Useful information

Moss Park, Ravenstone, Whithorn, Newton Stewart DG8 8DR
See website for details of performances | Admission sometimes free, otherwise ticket prices vary according to event | swallowtheatre.co.uk | 01988 850368

Monthly winter play readings Sun at 2pm | Admission free | See website for details

Getting there by public transport

The Swallow Theatre has rather tucked itself away from society but you can get within striking distance of it. Head for Stranraer railway station, at the end of the line from Glasgow Central. From the nearby ferry terminal, take the twice-a-day 416 bus (stagecoachbus.com; 01776 704484) to the junction of the A746 and the Castlewigg road. From there it's about a 2-mile stroll along a very minor road through Castlewigg and on to the theatre.

Tiny Cathedral
Cathedral of the Isles, Great Cumbrae

Conventional wisdom would have it that – laying spiritual considerations aside – the whole point of a cathedral is that it is grand. The cathedral is a symbol of majesty and power and, as such, demands to be built to a larger scale.

Just ask the Normans. When they wanted to make a statement to the Saxons in the north of England that the country was under new ownership, they threw up the colossal cathedral at Durham (making the benighted natives build most of it too). Three cheers then for the Cathedral of the Isles at Millport on the island of Great Cumbrae, for it has well and truly bucked the trend.

Britain's smallest cathedral had a rather modest start in life, as a collegiate chapel. When it was built in 1849 it was part of a small cluster of new buildings that housed a theological college belonging to the Scottish Episcopal Church. Its founder, George Frederick Boyle

(later the 6th Earl of Glasgow), had a vision that the seminary would become a 'new Iona'. He dreamt of a time when his island college would be considered as important to the Christianisation of 19th-century Scotland as St Columba's 6th-century island monastery had been to the establishment of the religion in the country.

As such, the complex at Great Cumbrae had to have a cathedral, and so the collegiate church – which had been designed by the famous gothic revival architect William Butterfield (whose work includes St Ninian's Cathedral in Perth) – was consecrated Cathedral of the Isles in 1876. Butterfield knew what he was doing and so it hardly matters that the building is not of the dimensions one might normally expect of a cathedral. Steeply pitched roofs, high walls of creamy-grey stone and a pencil-thin spire make a striking first impression.

The island on which this stirring edifice stands is yet to become a new Iona. Indeed, despite its size (about 4½ square miles), relatively large population (*c.* 1,400) and long tradition as a summer day-trip destination for thousands of Glaswegians, Great Cumbrae is little known outside Scotland. Sitting at the lower end of the Firth of Clyde, the island owes its prefix to the existence of a smaller neighbouring isle which goes by the name Little Cumbrae. The larger island is known to have been inhabited 12,000 years ago, at the end of the last Ice Age, but the first visitor whose name we know is St Mirin, who came here around AD 710. Taking a leaf out of St Patrick's book, he is said to have banished all snakes from the island (there certainly aren't any there now

so perhaps there's more to this Dark Ages serpent-banishing business than meets the eye). However, St Mirin is important to our story for a more prosaic reason: tradition dictates that the Cathedral of the Isles was built on the spot where he preached to the islanders.

As you go in, stop for a moment in the porch. There's a reminder here of the island's Christian heritage and the effect St Mirin had on the place: a gathering of Celtic crosses that were discovered during excavations in the 19th century. As you enter the cathedral proper, its smallness is made very apparent by the fact that there's only enough room in the nave to seat 80 people. The space is lit by a rainbow of coloured sunlight pouring through stained-glass windows. You should keep your eyes peeled for something one might not expect on a Scottish island: some Russian Orthodox icons. They're at the eastern end of the nave and were a gift to the cathedral in the late 19th century.

Steeply pitched roofs, high walls of creamy-grey stone and a pencil-thin spire make a striking first impression

In the chancel (the section that contains the altar), look up to see a ceiling beautifully decorated with depictions of ferns and wild flowers found on the island. There are also influences from two villages located rather further afield. The screen with its pillars made from Aberdeen granite was inspired by a church Butterfield had seen in the Essex village of Stebbing; while some colourful encaustic wall tiles echo medieval examples the architect had come across in Great Missenden, Buckinghamshire.

Rather than there being a pair of transepts (which would have given the cathedral a traditional crucifix-shaped floorplan), there's a Lady Chapel that shoots off further east of the chancel, giving the building a really stretched-out appearance. Opposite the chapel are college buildings that attach themselves to the cathedral towards the eastern end and include a cloister, the sort of detail that every self-respecting cathedral should possess.

You may notice too that the acoustics are really rather good. The building's relatively compact interior means that sound does not get lost in impossibly high domes and vaulted ceilings to echo there until the choirboys who sung the notes are halfway through a crafty ciggy behind the vestry. It's a feature the cathedral authorities are proud of, describing the acoustics as 'warm and resonant', qualities that make it attractive to choirs from the mainland.

If you're a lover of keyboards, this is definitely the place for you. The line-up here includes a restored organ that was built in 1867; a Bösendorfer concert grand piano; Richard Lipp and S & P Erard pianos; and, from 1976, a harpsichord, that most

punk rock of instruments. There's something else you might like to listen out for while you're at the Cathedral of the Isles – the chimes of the clock. If you want to know the time, be sure to listen well: while the bells mark each quarter hour, there is actually no clock face. It's an unorthodox set-up and there's probably a metaphor buried at the heart of it. Or more likely, given the location, a sermon illustration.

Useful information

College Street, Millport, Isle of Cumbrae, North Ayrshire KA28 0HE

Open daily 8.30am–6pm | Daily services: Morning Prayer 8.30am, Evening Prayer 5.45pm; Sun only: Sung Eucharist 11am | Admission free (though no donation is asked for, no doubt it would be appreciated) cathedraloftheisles.org | 01475 530353

Getting there by public transport

From Largs railway station, the terminus of a line from Glasgow Central, make your way the short distance along Main Street to the ferry terminal. Board one of the frequent ferries (calmac.co.uk; 0800 066 5000) for the 10-minute journey to Great Cumbrae. A bus that connects with the ferry takes passengers down to Millport at the southern end of the island. From Glasgow Street, which runs along the shore, find College Street, which is between the Newton Bar and the Garrison grounds and more or less cuts the long thin village in two. Go gently upwards along College Street, past George Street to the cathedral grounds, entered by a fancy gateway to your right.

Tiny Coffins
The Fairy Coffins of Arthur's Seat, Edinburgh

The world is an unpredictable place. When a group of young boys went out rabbiting one June day on Arthur's Seat – the extinct volcano that glowers down at the city of Edinburgh – they could not possibly have known that they'd return with a bizarre trove that would still have everyone guessing at its meaning over 180 years later.

While searching burrows somewhere on the hill (the precise spot is not known), one of the posse of children noticed three slabs of slate in an unnaturally straight line covering the opening of a little crevice. What he found there were 17 minute coffins, each one filled with a tiny figurine dressed as for the grave.

He and his friends then did what any self-respecting group of boys would do – they picked up the coffins and started throwing them at one another, taking them for 'unmeaning and contemptible trifles' as the report in *The Scotsman* was later to put it. On account of this will to violence in the young male, nine

wooden corpses and their coffins were lost.

On 20 July 1836 a report of the discovery was published in *The Times*, which in those days was the newspaper of record. A gentleman named Charles Fort, well known for his investigations into the paranormal, described the find in a terse style reminiscent of Dan Brown at his most lyrical:

> *Little cave. Seventeen tiny coffins. Three or four inches long. In the coffins were miniature wooden figures. They were dressed differently in both style and material. There were two tiers of eight coffins each, and a third one*

begun, with one coffin…In the first tier, the coffins were quite decayed, and the wrappings had moldered [sic] away. In the second tier, the effects of age had not advanced so far. And the top coffin was quite recent looking.

As soon as news of the unearthing of this macabre collection spread, the nation began to buzz with theories as to who put it there, when they put it there and what it might signify.

The Scotsman put its money on some sort of dark magic being at play. Witches, they asserted, had buried the coffins in order to cast a spell for some unknown but doubtless hideous purpose. Others claimed that the figures represented sailors lost at sea or miscarried babies, though there was nothing to back this up beyond

fancy. They are certainly not the product of an expert woodworker.

The bodies themselves are primitive little things. There's some detailing on the faces and feet, but some are missing an arm, apparently prised off to make the corpse fit into the coffin. Some are wearing clothes that have been stitched but with no attempt to make the apparel look attractive.

The coffins, meanwhile, are all made from solid pieces of Scots pine that had a cavity hollowed out of them. Although all are roughly the same length, they vary somewhat as to their other dimensions, each one being between 0.7in and 1.2in wide and roughly an inch deep. They all have a lid that was held down crudely by a number of brass pins or pieces of wire. The sides and the lids are

festooned with little pieces of tin in some attempt at ornamentation. So far, so curious.

However, there has been a scientific study made into the coffins and their occupants. Respected academics Allen Simpson and Samuel Menefee wrote up their findings in *The Book of the Old Edinburgh Club*, the journal of the Scottish capital's local history society. The conclusion they drew as to the age of the coffins and the clothing found within was that they were all of early 19th-century origin and probably dated from around 1830, so the likelihood is that they had not been lying up on Arthur's Seat for all that long before the boys found them. Intriguingly, they also discovered that the tin used for decorating the coffins was similar to that used at the time for shoe buckles, which makes it possible that they were the work of a shoemaker.

The bodies are all pretty much the same size – in stark contrast to the coffins – and some may have had hats that were removed. This suggests that

Was the tiny burial spot on Arthur's Seat created as a memorial to those who lost their lives to Burke and Hare?

the figurines were made first and only later did the idea of burying them come to the maker (or makers – the study found that two people may have been involved). On discovering also that each of the miniature corpses could stand up on its own, Simpson and Menefee concluded that the bodies were probably toy soldiers (from the 1790s) who had had their muskets removed.

It is at this point that two notorious characters from the Edinburgh history books stroll onto the scene: 'resurrection men' William Burke and William Hare. The grave-robbing duo sold their newly disinterred corpses to medical men to use for anatomical research. When a gentleman called Donald died of natural causes in Hare's lodgings and the pair were able to sell him off straightaway, they gave up prowling the cemeteries for the recently dead (who were increasingly well protected by watchmen and so-called mortsafes) and decided to create a few fresh corpses of their own. They went on a killing spree, with their crimes coming to light in 1828. Significantly, after the selling of Donald, the pair are known to have murdered a further 16 people, bringing their tally to 17.

Was the tiny burial plot on Arthur's Seat a memorial to those who lost their lives to Burke and Hare? Or an attempt to give them, by proxy, the decent burial they were denied by going under the anatomist's knife? Perhaps the coffins were the work of a cobbler who knew the murderers and felt some guilt by association?

There's no concrete evidence beyond the coincidence in numbers and dates (and there's the difficulty of the bodies all being dressed like men when 12 of the victims were women) but this is the theory on which Simpson and Menefee have hung their respective hats.

The eight surviving coffins and their occupants are on permanent display at the National Museum of Scotland in the heart of Edinburgh. You can stare as long as you like at this eerie artefact from the city's history. Having done so, perhaps you can come up with your own theory as to why someone buried them on Arthur's Seat all those years ago.

Useful information

National Museum of Scotland: Chambers Street, Edinburgh EH1 1JF
Open daily 10am–5pm, Boxing Day and New Year's Day noon–5pm,
closed Christmas Day | Admission free (donations welcome)
nms.ac.uk | 0300 123 6789

Getting there by public transport

At Edinburgh Waverley, the Scottish capital's main railway station (and the only one in Britain partially named after a novel), take the Market Street exit, turn left and on reaching North Bridge shortly afterwards turn right. North Bridge becomes South Bridge and presently you'll come to Chambers Street on your right. Turn into it and the National Museum of Scotland is on your left. Arthur's Seat can be seen from almost anywhere in Edinburgh and can be climbed with relative ease by a well-worn path that starts near the Scottish Parliament building.

46

Tiny Submarines
The XT-craft of Aberlady Bay, East Lothian

It's not every beach that plays host to a piece of World War II history. Those that do usually confine themselves to hosting a tank trap or two, detritus that somehow missed being cleared away when the threat of invasion had passed. Those mighty blocks of concrete are often impressively large but the story they tell is limited to their participation in an event that thankfully did not come to pass.

The wide caramel sands of Aberlady Bay, on the other hand, are the unlikely last resting place of two relics of quite a different order.

Roughly 17 miles along the coast from Edinburgh, Aberlady is a pleasant little village, quite at odds with the image suggested by the meaning of its Gaelic name, Obar Lobhtach ('rotten river mouth'). There's been a harbour here at the outflow of Peffer Burn since the 7th century or possibly earlier and, as one of the few places where a boat could put in on this sandy coastline, the community grew to some importance in the Middle Ages as a base for fishing and whaling

vessels. To the north are extensive sand dunes, crossed by a boardwalk about half a mile to the east of the village. Beyond the dunes lies Aberlady Bay and, at low tide, a vast expanse of beach, roughly in the shape of a triangle, called Gullane Sands. In 1952 the area became the very first Local Nature Reserve in the UK and today it's also a Site of Special Scientific Interest. The quality of the birdwatching on offer upon the 1,400 acres of sand, saltmarsh and mudflats can be judged by the fact that the Scottish Ornithologists' Club has chosen to base its headquarters overlooking the bay.

And far out across the beach, almost at the low-tide line, is a bulky concrete block. Flanking it are a couple of rather more indistinct shapes, as if two large slugs had fetched up there – at the bottom of the second 'l' of 'Gullane Sands' as it appears on the Ordnance Survey Landranger map no. 66. These are the wrecks of two midget submarines.

There has been some debate in the past about whether they are X-craft submarines, which were used in operations during World War II, or XT-craft, which were very similar but used only as training vessels. However, after thorough inspections and consultation with experts at the Royal Navy Submarine Museum in Gosport, it has been confirmed that they are both the training version. On reflection, this is hardly surprising since so many of the operational vessels were lost at sea or destroyed by enemy fire.

After a year's development at a secret base on the Isle of Lewis, the first X-craft were launched in 1943. They were designed to surprise the enemy by getting into ports and harbours that had been made inaccessible to larger submarines by the use of booms and netting. The submarines were just 52ft long, not quite 6ft wide and just over 5ft high.

Their three- or four-man crews must have been very cramped – it was certainly not a posting for anyone with claustrophobia –and only short men were selected to serve in them. The fact that there was only one way out of the submarine cannot have raised morale, and indeed this design fault was to prove fatal.

Although they were designed to sail for 1,200 miles underwater at a top speed of 6 knots, typically they would be towed or transported to within striking distance of their target by an ordinary submarine. The X-crafts' 'passage crews' would then change places with the vessels' 'attack crews' who would be responsible for approaching the objective, attaching high explosive charges to it, setting off the timed fuses, and getting away as best they could.

Although these midget submarines were to play a strategic role in the Normandy landings, the main task assigned to them was to attack German battleships based along the Norwegian coastline. The presence of these behemoths of the ocean in western Scandinavia threatened Allied shipping in the North Sea and thus tied down a great many Royal Navy ships in protective duties. One particular thorn in the Allies' side was the KMS *Tirpitz*, a battleship so enormous it had a crew of over 2,000 and guns that could fire shells 22 miles, sinking ships before their crews had any idea they were in danger.

Three X-craft were despatched to attempt to sink the *Tirpitz* while it lay up in Kåfjord on the Norwegian coast. One of the three managed to get beneath the ship, set its charges and move away. The explosions are said to have lifted the *Tirpitz* 6ft clear of the water. She took in a great deal of seawater but was not sunk. However, the battleship was put out of commission for six months, a fact that the Germans managed to hide from the Allies. Half of the 12 crewmen involved in the attack lost their lives and the other half were captured. This was far from unusual. Misadventures during the missions the X-craft were sent on were numerous and the loss of life of their crews was tragically high.

The attempt to sink the *Tirpitz* was captured in the 1955 British film *Above Us The Waves*, starring John Mills and Donald Sinden.

So, how did two World War II midget submarines come to be spending their last days rusting away on a beach on the east coast of Scotland? Only six XT-craft midget submarines were ever manufactured (all by Vickers) and some reports still claim today that they were all scrapped in 1945 having served their purpose. However, we know that at least two survived to May 1946, because these are the ones now lying on the Gullane Sands. Their end was rather ignominious. They were towed to the spot where they now lie, tethered to a concrete tank trap about 200yd apart, and used as targets by Seafire and Mosquito aeroplanes in order to test out various forms of ammunition.

The submarines are not the only wrecks in Aberlady Bay. There are also eight fishing vessels marooned, washed over by the tides and slowly rotting to nothing. They're all much older

> The submarines are not the only wrecks in Aberlady Bay. There are also eight fishing vessels marooned, washed over by the tides and slowly rotting to nothing

than the submarines, dating from the 19th or early 20th centuries, and have been officially designated as scheduled ancient monuments. But it's the XT-craft that send a shiver down the spine. They were naturally knocked about by the target practice and age has withered them, as they have been exposed to the vicissitudes of the North Sea for over 70 years. However, the two vessels remain recognisable as miniature submarines, with the more southerly of the two noticeably better preserved. It's a shame that they were not kept intact as a tribute to the bravery of the men who sailed in them and a reminder of the sheer awfulness of war, but at least their presence on the sands at Aberlady Bay means that the service their crews rendered is not completely forgotten.

NB The submarines are only visible at low tide. Do not touch them. Adhere to the age-old saying: take only photos and leave only footprints. Also, check tide times and take great care to get back to the shore before the tide begins to come back in, as it does so very swiftly on this part of the coast. If in doubt, stay on the shore and come back another day – the submarines aren't going anywhere.

Useful information

Aberlady Bay, near Aberlady, East Lothian

Getting there by public transport

Aberlady is easily accessible from Edinburgh. The frequent X5 bus (eastcoastbuses.co.uk) from Waterloo Place takes 55 minutes to reach the village. Alternatively, the 111 bus (prenticecoaches.co.uk; 01620 822620) from Drem railway station takes just 13 minutes to reach the same destination.

Tiny Harbour
Seacliff Harbour, East Lothian

Stand on the sandy beach at Seacliff and look around you and you'll find there's a host of things that attract your gaze. Out to sea stands the impressive Bass Rock, the remains of a volcano that blew its stack 320 million years ago and is turned a brilliant white each summer with the arrival of more than 100,000 gannets.

Closer at hand is the outline of Tantallon Castle, shooting up from a neighbouring clifftop like a discarded giant's comb that has lost most of its teeth. The coast is very pleasing on the eye too – rollers breaking on boat-gnawing rocks with innocent-looking grassy cliffs rising gently behind. Not for nothing was this coastline chosen by Robert Louis Stevenson for the novel *The Wrecker* that he co-wrote with his stepson. Relatives of the writer still live in the area today, though they restrict themselves to farming rather than wrecking (which, to be fair, is a pursuit more at home in fiction than fact).

Then there is the bay itself, a small cove dominated by lush red sandstone rock fashioned by the sea into all manner of surrealist sculptures – as if Picasso and Gaudí had each had a go at controlling the waves. One end is marked by a headland called Great Car, a jiggardly scrumble of boulders terminated by a rock called St Baldred's Boat with a white beacon with a cross on top – an exclamation mark at the end of an unruly sentence.

In the middle is a cave opposite a dainty outcrop of rock on the beach. At the western end sits a tidal islet called the Ghegan. A great wave-cut channel splits this mound in twain and the higher, larger portion has

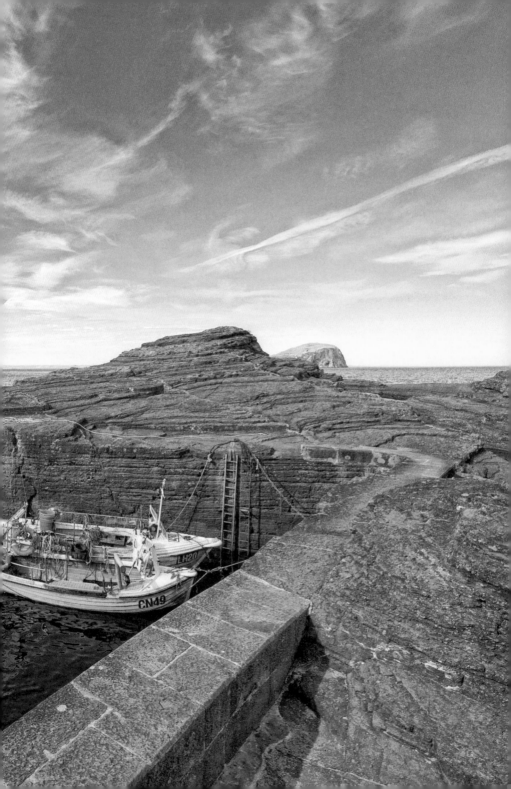

cultivated some grass on its rough plateau of a summit. But what you won't see is the cove's most remarkable feature. For that you will either have to scramble up onto the Ghegan or climb to the higher land behind the bay. Then you will notice that Seacliff has a secret – a minuscule hidden harbour hollowed out of the Ghegan's lower, smaller shard.

It really is a remarkable thing to behold. Britain's smallest harbour is not some makeshift haven rudely gouged out of the sandstone but a meticulously crafted affair whose walls have more in common with the dressed stone of a cathedral than the haphazard rock formations of the East Lothian coast.

It is not a harbour for those who have any doubt about their boat-handling skills though. A slim natural channel drives into the rock and a sharp turn to port is necessary to manoeuvre one's vessel into the extremely narrow entrance to the harbour, which is barely 9ft across.

> Four small lobster boats could just about cram themselves into the tiny dock if they went bow to aft and gunwale to gunwale

A winch, once used to open and close the harbour gate, stands rusted and obsolete above. There is no gate now, though the grooves in the rock where it used to sit are still clearly visible. Four small lobster boats could just about cram themselves into the tiny dock if they went bow to aft and gunwale to gunwale, though you'll be lucky if you see even one moored here today. You might catch the odd sea-kayaker gliding in for a nose about – the ease with which their small craft can pop in and out makes it a popular place for paddlers to explore on calm days. Divers doing training exercises may sometimes be spotted bobbing about in the water too. Royal Navy motorboats, on the other hand, would be far too large to dock here, though that didn't stop the much-loved Scottish author Nigel Tranter from taking some artistic licence to squeeze one in to aid the plot of his 1962 novel *Drug on the Market*.

The harbour sits in a spot that's surprisingly history-rich given how small and out of the way it is (North Berwick, the nearest town, is 3

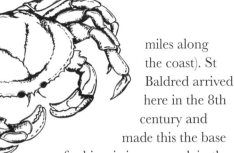

miles along the coast). St Baldred arrived here in the 8th century and made this the base for his missionary work in the area. This explains the naming of the Ghegan ('churchman's haven') as well as St Baldred's Boat (the rocky spur looks vaguely boat-like if you have a sufficiently elastic imagination). Over the centuries, the cove has proved a highly convenient place to marshal forces prior to the various assaults on Tantallon Castle. It was also felt necessary to guard it with soldiers during the Napoleonic Wars invasion scare (see page 117).

The outline of a ruined house nearby hints at a tragedy that struck here just over a century ago. The former residence was once a rather swish baronial pile and was designed in 1841 by David Bryce, one of the foremost architects of his day (his remoulding of the Bank of Scotland building appears on many a banknote today). The man who commissioned him was one George Sligo. Three decades later it passed into the hands of John Watson Laidlay, who had made his fortune in India from the production of indigo. In 1907 a fire broke out, gutting the building

and killing the then owner Andrew Laidlay.

Not long afterwards, the Royal Navy took an interest in the outbuildings, which had escaped damage. During World War I the navy transformed them into a top-secret base called HMS *Scottish Seacliff*. Here experimental techniques in defending shipping against attacks by U-boats were tried out.

But Seacliff harbour was the work of Andrew Laidlay, who lost his life here. In 1890 he had the innovative idea of setting up a steam engine on the rocks and using compressed air to cut down into them, which explains how the sandstone walls were carved so neatly. Back in the day there would have been plenty of action down in the tiny harbour. Little boats belonging to fishermen were moored here along with even smaller vessels whose owners fished for salmon with stake nets at the mouth of the River Tyne. Somehow, however, the calm that has descended on Seacliff

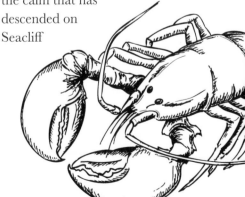

harbour rather suits the place – the lapping of the water against its walls as the tides rise and fall makes a fitting soundtrack for this secret little haven among the rocks.

Useful information

Seacliff, East Lothian

Always open | Admission free | A £3 charge is made for vehicular access to a nearby car park

Getting there by public transport

From North Berwick, the terminus of a line from Edinburgh Waverley, walk the short distance to Beach Road. There you can pick up a number 120 bus (eveinfo.co.uk; 01368 865500) which will take you for a 10-minute ride to the hamlet of Auldhame. A private road (which you can go on) leads to a car park and from there a track will take you to the shore. The harbour is at the western end of the beach.

Tiny World Championships
World Stone Skimming Championships, Argyll

There's something admirably inclusive about a world championships that anyone can enter for the cost of a pint and some crisps, and for which almost everyone will have the requisite abilities. After all, nearly everyone can throw a stone.

Of course, skimming a stone is a little trickier but it's a skill that can usually be picked up with a few minutes' practice. And that's just part of the reason why one of the world's smaller global competitions, the World Stone Skimming Championships, is also one of the most genial.

The setting for it is pretty impressive too. Easdale is one of the Slate Islands, a relatively little-visited group of isles off the west coast of Scotland. Their name comes from the colossal quantities of slate that have been quarried here and exported around the globe over the centuries (there's still a little quarrying being done today). The people of Easdale have long been proud of the fact that

they produced 'the slate that roofed the world'.

Easdale is only about 150yd off the coast of the Isle of Seil, which, though technically an island, looks like part of the mainland on a first glance at a map and is connected to it by a short crossing called, with a sly wink, the Bridge over the Atlantic. The small boat that sails from Seil to Easdale takes just 2 minutes to do so. On arrival at the tiny harbour, visitors are greeted by a compact village of attractive whitewashed houses and not a single road (each household has a wheelbarrow for transporting goods and chattels). Though only 25 acres in size, most of which is taken up with abandoned quarries, the island

has a thriving population of between 60 and 70, making it the smallest permanently inhabited island in the Inner Hebrides.

It is those abandoned quarries that make the island the perfect place to hold a stone-skimming championship. Most were left to be inundated by the sea and are now lagoons whose waveless surfaces make for ideal skimming conditions. Furthermore, there are countless little shards of slate simply lying about across the entire island – flat and light (but not too light)

projectiles that even the beginner can make sing across the water.

One particular flooded quarry, an incredibly picturesque little body of water lying just behind the village, is the site of the annual championships (motto: 'Skim your best, beat the rest!'). They take place on a Sunday every September, when the weather is still usually quite pleasant but after the time when such tourism as does take place on the island has subsided.

The first Easdale games took place in 1983, organised by a local man

named Albert Baker. They were such a success that it took until 1997 for the event to be run again when the community development group on Easdale resurrected Albert's idea as a fundraiser. This time the concept stuck and the competition has been held every year ever since, growing in popularity so that nowadays the event attracts around 350 participants.

To give everyone a chance, entrants are allotted their own group according to age and sex, which means that a whole host of world champions are crowned each year. The age categories are Adults (16–59), Juniors (10–15), Under 10s and (ahem) Old Tossers (60+). There's also a team prize in which the throws of all four members are added together.

Prizes for the winners come in the form of a cup, salvers, and even walking sticks (for the Old Tosser category) while there are medals made of slate (of course) for those coming second and third. A slate statuette of Albert Baker called 'The

One of the world's smaller global competitions, the World Stone Skimming Championships is also one of the most genial

Bertie' is also awarded to the best Easdale islander on the day.

The rules are kept mercifully simple. Each competitor stands on the official slate plinth and is allowed three attempts, with only their furthest skim counting. Stones can be no larger than 3in in diameter and must, of course, be of Easdale slate, untampered with in any way. A stone must bounce on the water at least three times and sink in a wide lane marked by buoys in order for it to be a legitimate throw. Judges at the side of the lagoon watch the stones assiduously to mark exactly where they finally disappear into the abyss so that they can measure the precise length each one has travelled (the number of bounces is immaterial, which is just as well because counting them can be a ticklish business).

Those who hit the back wall of the quarry (just over 200ft away) make it through to a 'Three Stone Toss-Off' in which the cumulative distance of their three tie-break throws is added up. And like all the best competitions, the last rule is: 'The judges' decision is final.'

It's probably a good idea to get in some practice on your own local lagoon beforehand if you want to give yourself a chance of doing well. The champion of the women's competition must usually hurl her projectile over 130ft. To win the men's event you'll have to hit the back wall with one of your three throws (eight men managed the feat in 2017) and back it up with three consistently long attempts in the Toss-Off.

The championships draw a truly international field, often with 30 or so countries involved. In 2017 the men's competition was won by Japanese skimthlete Keisuke Hashimoto (554ft for his three tie-breaker throws) with two Scots in second and third. The women's prize was taken home by the Swiss Nina Luginbuhl (144ft) with representatives from England and Hungary in the minor placings. Even the U10 boys event was won by an international competitor, a young Belgian man who bounced a stone a very creditable 92ft.

The competition has its own legends. It's a rare year when Englishwoman Lucy Wood of the Skimmy Latte team is not in the top three, and she often prevails over all her rivals; while Scotsman Dougie Isaacs has won the men's event no fewer than eight times (he was pushed back into second place in 2017).

But even if you're not a Lucy Wood or a Dougie Isaacs, the lengths of your three throws are sedulously recorded and posted onto the official World Stone Skimming Championships website (stoneskimming.com) for posterity.

Henceforth you can prove to any cynics and naysayers you come across that you have competed in a world championship finals.

For all this talk of rules and distances and winners, the event is intended primarily to be fun, just like the Olympics used to be in the good old days. On the Saturday night before the competition takes place there's a pre-skim party held in the Easdale Island Community Hall, an unexpectedly fantastic Gaudí-like building. The live acts include a band to dance to (expect something unusual such as a punk/bluegrass crossover). Films are shown for children, a barbecue is fired up and the bar is kept well stocked. There's many a finely tuned athlete who takes to the plinth the next day with a shocking hangover.

While you're visiting Easdale it would be criminal not to have a look in at a brace of tiny museums. Two minutes over the water at Ellenabeich, a village that stands on land reclaimed from the sea by Easdale's quarry spoil, there's the Slate Islands Heritage Centre and Museum which gives an insight into the quarries on Easdale, Belnahua, Luing and Seil.

On the isle itself, the single-room Easdale Island Folk Museum tells the story of the local people over the ages, in the days before their island home rivalled Olympia as the fulcrum of sporting excellence.

Useful information

Easdale Island, by Oban, Argyll PA34 4TB
Championships held annually on a weekend in Sep (see website for precise competition dates) | Entrance fees: Adult (16+) £5, 'Old Tossers' (60+) £3, Junior (10–15) £2, U10s £1 (team members pay an extra £1 each to be part of the team competition) | stoneskimming.com

Easdale Island Folk Museum: Open Apr–mid-Oct daily 11am–4pm (open in winter by arrangement) | Nominal charge easdalemuseum.org | 01852 300173

The Slate Islands Heritage Centre and Museum, Ellenabeich: Open Apr–Oct daily 10.30am–1pm and 2–5pm | Free | slateislands.org.uk

Getting there by public transport

Take the train to Oban, the terminus of a line from Glasgow Queen Street. From Stance 5 at the station board the number 18 bus (westcoastmotors. co.uk; 01586 552319) to Ellenabeich from where the ferry departs for the less than Odyssean voyage to Easdale. There are frequent sailings every day (but with a break at lunchtime, which seems fair enough, for we all must eat).

Tiny County
Clackmannanshire

Clackmannanshire may sound like one of those made-up counties beloved of the writers of works of fiction – take a bow Borsetshire, Barsetshire and Midsomer – but it's been an actual real county for over 700 years. Indeed, as one of Scotland's 33 historic counties it certainly has more right to the name than the leviathan that is Highland, the council area created in the 1970s that takes in the whole of northwest Scotland.

Covering just 61 square miles and with a population of a little over 50,000, Clackmannanshire is Britain's smallest proper county by some margin. However, 'The Wee County' – as it has been dubbed with leaden predictability – is well worth a dauner aboot. With its hills, castles, plucky little villages and abundant wildlife, in many ways it's a microcosm of the Scottish nation, albeit with the north bank of the River Forth standing in for a coastline.

The mountains are ably represented by the Ochil Hills, the southwestern

end of which grace the county and whose highest point, Ben Cleuch, is entirely claimed by Clackmannanshire. Coming in at a highly respectable 2,365ft, Ben Cleuch is a Graham rather than a Munro – it would need to be another 635ft high to qualify as the latter. However, it does compensate those who climb it with a cracking view from the summit. On a clear day (that most slippery of provisos), the vista to the south includes Edinburgh, the Forth bridges and Glasgow way over to the west; while to the north there's Ben Lomond, Ben Ledi and a range of other Southern Highlands peaks. If the weather isn't fine enough for such a panorama to be enjoyed, there is at least a stone shelter at the top where one can wait for the clouds to clear.

Clackmannanshire takes its name from the little-known town of Clackmannan. The community on the River Black Devon was also the county town up until 1822 when that honour made the short journey northwest to Alloa. The town's undoing was the silting up of its port on the Black Devon. Alloa, with its access to the far mightier Forth, grew at Clackmannan's expense and now boasts a population six times greater. For all that, or perhaps because of that, Clackmannan is a pleasant, rather old-fashioned place and its nearby castle, Clackmannan Tower, is a magnificent example of a 14th-century tower house. Perched on a hilltop and built of local sandstone by King David II, it's open to view at any time, though currently only from the outside.

Alloa, the town that took Clackmannan's throne, has its own tower, which is the largest surviving keep in the whole of Scotland. Fans of the admirably itinerant Mary, Queen of Scots will be pleased to learn she paid a visit once. Alloa Tower has some pretty impressive 18th-century decor within, walls 11ft thick, a solar dating from the Middle Ages and a view of nine counties (see 'clear day' above) from the top. The community that developed around it eventually became a town, one that grew in leaps and bounds during the Industrial Revolution, helped by its harbour, which had already made Alloa an important centre for trade.

The town is also the home of Alloa Athletic, a semi-professional football team that was founded in 1878 (beginning life as Clackmannan County). For over a hundred years 'The Wasps' endeavoured to achieve as little as possible beyond hopping back and forth between the lower divisions of Scottish league football and winning the local Stirlingshire

> With its hills, castles, plucky little villages and abundant wildlife, in many ways it's a microcosm of the Scottish nation

Cup from time to time. In 1999, the team forgot itself and won the Scottish Challenge Cup, a trophy devised specially for the lesser Scottish clubs so that not everything could be won by Celtic or Rangers. In the final they crushed Inverness Caledonian Thistle 5–4 on penalties after an entertaining 4–4 draw. Quite rightly, they've turned down the opportunity to win anything as prestigious since.

Despite its diminutive size, Clackmannanshire is home to half a dozen Hillfoots Villages, so called because they're all villages or small towns that lie in the shadow of the Ochil Hills. They're joined together by the Hillfoots Diamond Jubilee Way, a 13-mile footpath that follows the *Via Regia* or King's Highway that is mentioned in documents that go back to the 14th century and was probably used in the 16th century for royal journeys between Falkland Palace and Stirling Castle.

The small town of Dollar is probably the pick of the six communities, if largely because of the presence of yet another fortress – the early 15th-century Castle Campbell – which sits in the Dollar Glen, high on a hillside to the north. Inevitably, Mary, Queen of Scots paid a visit. More unusually, her host, the Protestant 5th Earl of Argyll, rebelled against her two years later. He joined her half-brother James Stewart and sundry other nobles who objected to Mary's marriage to the vain, violent and hard-drinking Lord Darnley. After a phoney war, contemptuously named the Chaseabout Raid on account of the failure of the two sides' forces to engage one another in battle, the rebels realised they were outnumbered and fled south to England. Castle Campbell duly surrendered to the queen and her consort.

Dollar also possesses a little museum, housed in a 19th-century woollen mill. Its exhibits tell the story of the town from prehistoric times (there's a pretty nifty Neolithic carved stone ball) to the days of the now sadly defunct Devon Valley Railway.

Thankfully, among all the castles and Neolithic stone balls there is a little room for wildlife. Northeast of Alloa lies the 370-acre Gartmorn Dam Country Park and Nature Reserve. Set around a huge reservoir that accounts for nearly half the park, Gartmorn Dam is alive with migrating wildfowl in winter, while many other birds live there all year round. It's something of an accidental haven for fauna since the reservoir was actually created as a power source to drive the pumps that kept the nearby Sauchie coalmines from flooding. So successful was the 17th-century project, carried out by Sir John Erskine, the 6th Earl of Mar, that it also helped kick-start the rise of Alloa as an industrial power in the region. Come for the whooper swans, goosander and teal, and stay for the ghostly clatter of power looms wafting up from the town below.

Useful information

Alloa Tower (National Trust for Scotland): Open Apr, Sep and Oct Fri–Mon noon–4pm | May–Aug Thu–Mon noon–5pm | Last entry 1 hour before closing| Adult £6.50, single adult family £11.50, family £16.50, concession £5| nts.org.uk| 01259 211701

Castle Campbell (Historic Environment Scotland): Open Apr–Sep daily 9.30am–5.30pm | Oct daily 10am–4pm | Nov–Mar Sat–Wed 10am–4pm Adult £6, children 5–15 £3.60, children U5s free, concession £4.80 historicenvironment.scot | 01259 742408

Dollar Museum: Open Easter–Christmas Sat 11am–1pm and 2–4.30pm, Sun 2–4.30pm | Admission free | clacks.gov.uk/visiting/dollarmuseum 01259 742895

Gartmorn Dam Country Park and Nature Reserve: clacks.gov.uk/culture/gartmorndam/| 01259 450000

Getting there by public transport

Rejoice, for Alloa railway station reopened (a little to the east of its previous incarnation) in 2008, 40 years after its closure. It makes Clackmannanshire easily accessible by rail because Alloa is the terminus on a line that takes in Stirling and Glasgow. It's possible to take buses to all the major fleshpots of Clackmannanshire, including Yetts o' Muckhart, a hamlet in the distant northeast of the county.

50

Tiny Cave
St Fillan's Cave, Kingdom of Fife

Some players on history's stage are doomed to have the truth about their brief time upon it drowned in a mire of mythology. Good King Wenceslas is a prime example; Queen Boudicca another (and, to rub salt into the wound, we habitually get her name wrong).

To that list we can add poor St Fillan. Although there's no doubt that the 8th-century Irish missionary to the heathen Picts did actually exist – he was the grandson of a King of Leinster no less – pretty much everything he did in his life has been overshadowed by the rather ridiculous legends that have been attached to him. And the most ridiculous legend of all concerns the bizarre method employed to bring light to the cave in which he worked.

But before we get to that, and the otherwise fantastic cave itself, it behoves us to examine what we do actually know about the man. He came from Munster, the son of Kentigerna, a princess who also

found sainthood. After entering monastic life, Fillan joined his mother and other close family members in a mission to the heathen Picts of Scotland in AD 717. He ended up at Pittenweem, a fishing village on the east coast of Scotland, eventually becoming abbot of a monastery in the area.

So much for the facts. Like many a saint, Fillan has been credited with miraculous healing powers, particularly with regard to illnesses that effect the mind. Right up to the 19th century, those deemed to be so afflicted were dipped in a pool that bears his name, tethered to a font and left to stew overnight. The victim was adjudged to have been cured if, come the morning, they were no longer tied up. The mental health of those who meted out this barbarism was apparently not an issue.

There's also a story about a wolf killing an ox that Fillan was using to plough a field near Killin (home to a church dedicated to the saint) in Stirlingshire. The wolf was miraculously coerced into doing the work of the ox.

However, the most ludicrous tale involves the little cavity in a rock in Pittenweem now known as St Fillan's Cave. Coming across the tiny cavern, the eponymous saint is said to have seen its possibilities as a place for peaceful study. However, as the day wore on and the light became crepuscular, the saint could no longer see to read or write. He petitioned God on the matter and, for answer, his left arm was made luminous. Rather than scaring the life out of him, which in the circumstances would have been an understandable reaction, Fillan said

his thanks and henceforth was never without light when he needed to work on a sermon. Why he could not have lit a torch, as anyone else might have done, is not a question that is ever addressed. Thinking differently is doubtless all part and parcel of being a saint.

But none of that makes his cave any less delightful to visit. The charm starts with its very location. It's not on the coast facing the sea (see page 283) or high up on a hillside (see page 34) but at the side of a broad path in Pittenweem. Those who are up on their Pictish and Scottish Gaelic will know that 'Pit' comes from the Pictish *pett* signifying 'place', while 'enweem' is a corruption of the Gaelic *na h-Uaimh* meaning 'of the caves'.

A sort of rustic stone porch has been built around the narrow entrance, which is further guarded by an iron gate emblazoned with a Celtic cross. Unlocking this (see below for details on securing the key), you pass along a short passage

You'll also see a little pool created by the water that drips and plops through the space, carving out fresh niches and hollows in the cavern with infinitesimal patience

into a small chamber where there is an information board. Another passageway beyond leads to the main cavern, which is of no great size either, but which has been converted into a chapel. A floor of stone flags has been laid down and at one end there stands a simple stone altar. Some steps lead up to a further tunnel that comes out into a garden, but nowadays this is blocked off by a gate.

There's a spring and a well in the cave, which would certainly have made it an attractive place to work. When you visit you'll also see a little pool created by the water that drips and plops through the space, carving out fresh niches and hollows in the cavern with infinitesimal patience. The walls are also worth investigating – they're a patchwork of endlessly evolving patterns with hues and tones that range from creams, greys and browns to the rich red of iron ore.

All in all, it's a tremendously peaceful place. The clamour of the world outside is dulled and you can be still in a space where the constant demands on your senses are abated for a moment.

St Fillan isn't the only holy person believed to have spent time here. For many years, a chat with the cave's hermit-in-residence-du-jour seems to have been part of the ritual of a pilgrimage to St Andrews. At other times the little cavern is also believed to have been used by a local monastery; by fishermen as a store; by smugglers to hide their illicit goods (for what cave worth its salt hasn't?); as a lock-up for suspected witches (Pittenweem hosted some notorious witch trials); and as a rubbish dump. This last application is certainly true, because the cave is known to have disappeared completely beneath the collected detritus. It was cleared out in 1935 and rededicated to St Fillan, but it wasn't until 2000 that it was opened to the public.

Despite not being one of the better known saints, Fillan does have various churches dedicated to him and a valley, Strath Fillan, in western Perthshire. He's even swung his own village. St Fillans – like St Davids (see page 174) a community that has been careless about its apostrophe – sits at the eastern end of Loch Earn in the Central Highlands of Scotland. What the saint would have made about the local belief in the existence of fairies can only be imagined. The wee folk are said to live under one particular rock in a nearby field where St Fillan once set up some sort of homestead. In November 2005, the rock was endangered by a developer's diggers. Residents protested so vigorously that

the fairies would be killed if their homes were disturbed that plans for a housing estate on the site were shelved.

One can't help thinking that had St Fillan known that his mission to the Picts would result in a legend about him having a luminous arm, a conviction that fairies live where he set up camp, and a pool that could cure trussed-up mentally ill patients, he might well have tried to persuade God to let him stay in Ireland. Still, at least he's left us with a pretty cool cave.

Useful information

Cove Wynd, Pittenweem, Kingdom of Fife KY10 2LE
The key is held at Pittenweem Chocolate Company and Cocoa Tree Café (which incidentally makes an excellent place to repair to after the excitement of the cave), just around the corner on Pittenweem High Street | The café is open daily 10am–6pm except Christmas Day and New Year's Day
Admission £1 per person (proceeds to the Episcopal Church)
pittenweemchocolate.co.uk | 01333 311495
The cave is owned by the Bishop Low Trust and cared for by St John's Scottish Episcopal Church in Pittenweem.
NB Don't forget to take a torch.

Getting there by public transport

Jump on the train to Kirkcaldy (pronounced 'Kirkuddy') on the line heading up the east coast of Scotland from Edinburgh Waverley. Stroll past the town's museum and through the pleasant Kirkcaldy War Memorial Gardens to its southeastern corner and St Brycedale Avenue.

Outside the Adam Smith Theatre you can pick up an X60 bus (stagecoachbus.com; 01383 660880) which takes about an hour to get to Viewforth Place in Pittenweem. From there it's a short walk along South Loan to the High Street. Turn left (picking up the key from the Cocoa Tree Café) and look for the entrance to Cove Wynd just to the right of St John's church. The cave is a short distance along the broad pathway.

51

Tiny House
The Scottish Crannog Centre, Perthshire

Imagine for a moment that you lived in the past. Not the recent past – nobody in their right mind would want to live through the 1820s again, although admittedly it would probably have been quite something to read the first reports that the Rosetta Stone had been translated – but the very distant past. Let's say a few thousand years ago. Where would you build your home? And how would you defend it against wild animals or, worse still, wild humans?

For many people in Ireland and Scotland, the answer was to construct a crannog. It was a very labour-intensive venture but the rewards were handsome. Building one involved hauling rocks into a loch or lake until they broke the surface to create an artificial island, or using sturdy tree trunks as piles to ram into a high point in the loch bed so that a platform could be erected above the surface. Whichever method you chose would enable you to build a tiny roundhouse in a place where the water that surrounded it would act as a natural protective barrier. So successful was this means of establishing a relatively safe base for one's family or wider social group that crannogs were built in Ireland and Scotland (and very occasionally in Wales too) from about 3000 BC right up to the 17th century. Several hundred have been discovered in Scotland, so the next time you look over a loch and spot a minuscule circular tree-covered island, you may well be looking at a crannog.

No house on a crannog has survived the intervening years but

269

a fantastically precise reconstruction at the Scottish Crannog Centre on Loch Tay does give us a good idea of what they looked like and what it was like to live in one. It was completed in 1996 by the Scottish Trust for Underwater Archaeology to highlight that part of Scotland's heritage that lurks below the surface of the water. They replicated as closely as possible the sort of crannog that would have been common in the Early Iron Age, basing their assumptions on sub-aqua research they'd done on an actual crannog in Loch Tay.

Consequently, it's composed of the same materials – mostly timber and brush – that would have been available to the people back then. It was largely built without the help of modern technology, so the 30ft alder and oak piles had to be driven into the loch bed by hand, which was apparently as tricky and as physically taxing as it sounds. The crannog and roundhouse, with its walls of hazel woven into hurdles, floor of young alders lashed or pegged together, and roof of reed thatch rising to a point in the centre at an angle that would have dispersed both rain and snow, are as authentic a reproduction of the loch-based homes built 2,500 years ago as one could hope to visit. However,

in case you have a yen to build your own someday, it should be noted that there's a possibility that bracken, rushes and straw were used to thatch the roof back in the day, though no one can be absolutely sure about that.

A crannog was not just a home for the family. In cold weather or times of danger, animals would have been kept inside too and archaeological evidence suggests that they had a space made specifically for them just inside the door. This would have made the atmosphere inside the house somewhat ripe (though with fish and meat also hanging up inside perhaps Iron Age families were inured to that) but would also have helped to heat the space, which, in the depths of winter, would certainly have been a compensation. A fire, laid on a circle of clay, would also have helped in this regard, with the smoke infiltrating the high thatch above rather than choking everyone half to death. The remainder of the area is divided up using internal moveable walls made of hazel to provide sleeping and living areas. A timber walkway links the homestead to the shore. In some crannogs, this walkway would be hacked away with an axe and possibly also set alight at the approach of a potential enemy.

There's a little museum too, where you can gaze upon items recovered from the so-called Oakbank Crannog that sat on Loch Tay sometime between 600 and 400 BC. The astonishing array of artefacts that one would have supposed had rotted away long since includes a plough, the paddle of a canoe, some jewellery, a collection of utensils used around the home and even a piece of cloth made from wool that was spun by hand. After a saunter around the museum and a tour around the crannog (with a guide bravely decked out in replica clothing of the time), there's a chance to see some Iron Age technology in action. Experts in their craft will take you through the intricacies of how grain was ground to make flour; how holes were drilled in stones; how wool was spun; and how fire was made by means of a wooden drill. Best of all, you can try your hand yourself to see how you'd have got on had you been born to a happy Iron Age couple. And who knows? With global warming marching on apace, these kind of skills may one day come in handy.

Useful information

Loch Tay, Kenmore, Nr Aberfeldy, Perthshire PH15 2HY
Open daily Apr–Oct 10am–5.30pm (last tour 4.15pm) | Adult £10, senior £9, student (17+) £9, child (5–16) £7, family (2+2) £32
crannog.co.uk | 01887 830583
NB Allow 1–2 hours for a visit. All-day events may be more expensive.

Getting there by public transport

Take the train to Dunkeld and Birnam railway station on the line between Perth and Inverness. On the Perth Road, opposite Birnam Hotel, hop on a number 23 bus (stagecoachbus.com; 01738 629339) to Breadalbane Community Campus in Aberfeldy. From there you'll have to take a taxi the final 6½ miles or time it just right and you can grab the schooldays-only 893 bus (dochertysmidlandcoaches.co.uk | 01764 662218) which leaves at 3.45pm and will speed you all the way to the museum.

52

Tiny Distillery
Edradour, Perthshire

Aah, whisky. Tis a spirit over which folk either wax lyrical or greet by extending the tongue from the mouth and making an anguished noise like a sheep vomiting up a thistle. The latter response is not so often heard in Scotland, of course, where it is illegal to disparage the national drink, a crime that carries a minimum sentence of five years of ostracism.

The various attributes of any one whisky hang on a vast number of differentials. The qualities of the water used are, of course, of great importance, as is the type and calibre of the malted barley. However, as any distiller will tell you, there are myriad other factors involved that give each whisky its own particular taste. One of these factors, perhaps surprisingly, is the actual size of the still in which the whisky is produced.

In this respect Edradour (Scottish Gaelic for 'the land between two rivers') is singular indeed. Not only is it Scotland's smallest whisky distillery, it also uses the smallest stills

of any whisky distillery in the land. As whisky expert Michael Jackson (different one) points out, 'Edradour is the last original "farm" distillery … its stills are the smallest in Scotland and that must contribute to the distinctive richness of the malt.'

So how did this tiny little distillery not far from the centre of Scotland come into being and how is it still around when every other farm-based distillery has fallen by the wayside?

For answers to those questions we need to step back in time. Exactly to what point in time is unclear since there are several competing versions of the early history of whisky in

Scotland. Many point to Friar John Cor as the country's first distiller, since he is recorded as being ordered to produce eight bottles of the spirit for King James IV in 1495. Others opine that the story goes way back before then, and that the sacred knowledge of whisky-making was brought over by Irish missionaries in the 6th century. Some even claim that the Vikings were the first distillers in Scotland, having picked up the skill while fighting as mercenaries in the Arab–Byzantine wars.

Whichever story is true, what we do know is that for hundreds of years the production of whisky outwith the monasteries was very largely a domestic affair, carried out on crofts and usually distributed locally among families and neighbours. In the Highlands, not a great deal changed when attempts were made to tax the spirit. Indeed, the Scottish Excise Act of 1644 saw the government fall foul of the law of unintended consequences. By increasing the duty on whisky they simply encouraged a wider proliferation of illegal stills.

It was only when a further Excise Act in 1823 reduced the duties payable that the conditions were created in which it was worthwhile for stills to become licensed operators. Two years later, a group of farmers got together, formed a cooperative and established the Edradour distillery (though under the name Glenforres). The operation moved to the company's present location just outside the small town of Pitlochry 11 years later.

Over the decades, the distillery changed hands and began to make something of a name for itself. So much so that it attracted the attention of the American Mafia. In 1938, Irving Haim, the agent of Mafia capo Frank Costello, bought a substantial shareholding in the distillery. Three years later, in an incident unrelated to the Mob, Edradour became even more famous. The SS *Politician* ran aground off the island of Eriskay

Edradour is the last original 'farm' distillery ... its stills are the smallest in Scotland and that must contribute to the distinctive richness of the malt in the Western Isles, disgorging her cargo of 28,000 cases of whisky, many of which came from the Pitlochry distillery. The story of the wreck was captured in Compton Mackenzie's novel *Whisky Galore*, which was turned into a popular Ealing comedy of the same name (but with an added exclamation mark) starring Basil Radford, Joan Greenwood and a youthful Gordon Jackson.

And all this time the distillery had been powered by a watermill. Only in 1947 was electricity installed. The company changed hands yet more times (and lost its Mafia connection), was caught in a flash flood, was bought by a man named Andrew Symington – the first Scot to own the company for many a year – and continued to introduce new whiskies such as 2003's Ballechin (heavy on the peat) and 2013's 18-year-old Edradour single malt.

There's a very smart visitor centre and tasting bar at the distillery so you can go on a tour to see how it's all done and sample a wee dram afterwards. Nowadays, all the whisky

is matured and bottled on site, so visitors get to observe the whole operation from raw ingredients to finished product. Unlike in most distilleries nowadays, there's not a single computer used in the process, which itself has changed very little since the days of the original Edradour farmers.

There is good news too for those for whom whisky elicits the aforementioned sheep/thistle response but who enjoy a good wine. The distillery now produces various whiskies that have spent some time maturing in casks of Marsala, Bordeaux and Barolo to give them a wine finish. And if that's still too whisky-like, they also do a cream liqueur. Enjoy responsibly.

Useful information

A little to the northeast of Pitlochry, Perthshire PH16 5JP
Open end Mar–near end Oct Mon–Sat 10am–5pm, last tour at 4pm
(tours last an hour) | Near end Oct–end Mar Mon–Fri 10am–4.30pm,
last tour at 3pm | Closed around 21 Dec–7 Jan | Adult £10, children
(12–17) £5, children under 12 not admitted, booking required for groups
of 8 or more   edradour.com | 01796 472095

Getting there by public transport

Pitlochry railway station is on the rather eye-pleasing line between
Perth and Inverness. Buses won't get you much closer to the distillery
so you might as well make use of a delightful waymarked circular walk
(3 miles in total) to Edradour from Atholl Road in Pitlochry. Details
can be found on noticeboards in the town and from Pitlochry's Tourist
Information Centre (now called an iCentre because it's trendy) on Atholl
Road (01796 472215)

53

Tiny Castle
Edzell Castle, Angus

Of all the epithets that can be applied to a family, 'carefree' is surely one to be cherished the most. The '*lichtsome*' (i.e. carefree) Lindsays' lived at a time and place when to be free of care was a rare pleasure indeed. Scotland in the mid to late Middle Ages was a place of almost constant upheaval and uncertainty, which is not the most fertile soil from which to bring forth peace of mind, a full stomach or a long life. It took its toll on the lichtsome Lindsays as well.

The potted history of the family provided by Historic Environment Scotland, who care for Edzell Castle, also describes them as 'turbulent and tragic'. For all that they appeared to live in clover, to be a Lindsay was often not a bed of roses.

It's ironic then that their lasting legacy has been a wonderful formal garden known as the Pleasance, a monument far more impressive than the fragment of their modest castle that remains. And yet without the castle there would be no garden, so it's only right to celebrate them both.

Edzell Castle stands at the foot of the Hill of Edzell, between the rivers West Water and North Esk. Little remains of the first fortress built to defend this potential gateway into the Highlands. That was thrown up in the 1100s as a motte-and-bailey affair and was made of timber. The Crawford Lindsays bought it up around the middle of the 14th century but it wasn't until the 1520s that they started work on a stone castle close by to replace it. They built what is known as the Tower House, with extensions to it coming along in later decades. The fabulous walled garden was added in 1604 by David, Lord Edzell. Although called a castle, it never amounted to much more than a fortified residence, though it was considered grand enough for Mary, Queen of Scots to pay a visit in 1562 (when David would have been just 11 or 12, though by then he had already been laird of Edzell for four years). Her son, James VI of Scotland (later also James I of England), stayed twice. Such visits, while a great honour, were a burden financially – putting up a monarch and entourage was not something one could do on the cheap.

Should you pay a visit yourself (the cost is now borne by the guest rather than the host but is rather more reasonable than of old), you'll first notice the simple L-shaped Tower House, the vivid pink of its red sandstone walls providing a contrast to the lush parkland and verdant farmland by which the castle is surrounded. Further rooms for the family are ranged along a courtyard in a less imposing building built on Sir David's orders.

> It never amounted to much more than a fortified residence, though it was grand enough for Mary, Queen of Scots to pay a visit in 1562

Do have a look at the summer house too. It was created at the same time as the garden so that the family and their guests might enjoy a banquet and perhaps some alfresco entertainment away from the confines of the main house. Behind the castle lies the large sumptuous garden with its 12ft-high walls on three sides and a lower wall on the fourth, forming an enclosed space full of the geometrical joys of a formal parterre garden.

Unique joys, as it happens, since the three high walls are ornamented with a combination of stone reliefs you'll not see in another garden anywhere. One wall is devoted to depictions of the seven cardinal virtues, another shows the seven planetary deities, while the third is concerned with the seven liberal arts. They were copied from prints that Sir David had brought back from Germany, one of the many countries he visited on educational tours.

This last wall is a celebration of the Renaissance – the arts in question being Arithmetica, Astronomia, Dialectica, Geometria, Grammatica, Musica and Rhetorica. These encompass the whole gamut of liberal education in the great universities of Europe in the early 17th century. The panel portraying Astronomia has sadly vanished, but the other six are still in situ. The seven planetary deities can be viewed in the summer house (where they are kept to protect them from the damaging effects of the weather).

The seven virtues – rather less well known than the seven deadly sins – are Charity, Faith, Fortitude, Hope, Justice, Prudence and Temperance. If they do not seem quite as well executed as the other panels, that may be because David Lindsay had

rather overstretched himself, fiscally speaking, what with the garden and the summer house (and a bath house too). There's every chance he commissioned a lesser craftsman to knock these seven off at a bargain rate just so he could get the garden finished. He died in 1610, so did not have long to enjoy the fruits of his expenditure. It's said that in the midst of life we are in debt – and that was certainly true of his surviving family, who were bequeathed a wonderful garden and attendant buildings, but were plunged deep into the red at the same time.

It's surprising that the Lindsays managed to hold things together for another century or so. Eventually, though, their fortunes took a turn for the worse and they were forced to sell Edzell Castle in 1715, that most momentous of dates in Scottish history. The man they sold it to, the Earl of Panmure, joined the first Jacobite Rebellion that year and before he had even had time to change the wallpaper, Edzell was confiscated from him as punishment for his supposed treachery. It was to be the undoing of the castle and marked the beginning of its decline into ruination. The estate fell into the hands of the York Buildings Company, a sort of 18th-century asset stripper which went bankrupt about 50 years later. Pretty much everything of value was then ripped out and sold on behalf of the company's creditors.

Thankfully, the property was handed to HM Office of Works in the 1930s and the Pleasance was returned to the splendour it had enjoyed under the lichtsome family that created it. To enjoy it at its best, drop by in early July, when the bedding plants are in full bloom. Listen closely and perhaps you'll even hear a spectral Lindsay give an approving sniff of the floral scents wafting through the air.

Useful information

Edzell, by Brechin, Angus DD9 7UE
Open Apr–Sep daily 9.30am–5.30pm, October daily 10am–4pm
Adult £6, children (5–15) £3.60, U5s free, concession £4.80
historicenvironment.scot | 01356 648631
NB Children under 16 must be accompanied by an adult.

Getting there by public transport

Laurencekirk in Aberdeenshire is the nearest railway station to Edzell but unless you want to walk or cycle 11 miles, you'll have to travel instead to Montrose on the line between Dundee and Aberdeen. From Montrose High Street take the number 39 bus to Stracathro Hospital (by the porter's lodge) where you can change to the 21 bus (both stagecoachbus. com; 01383 660880) which will take you to the Tuck Inn (ho ho) on Edzell High Street. Stroll back along the High Street and turn left into Lethnot Road. Walk for just under a mile and you'll come to the entrance to Edzell Castle on your right.

54

Tiny Cave
The Massacre Cave, Inner Hebrides

Anyone who has read much Scottish history could be forgiven for thinking that the word 'interminable' had been created specifically to describe Highland clan feuds. MacDonalds were always fighting Campbells, the Johnstones were constantly at dirks drawn with the Maxwells, and pretty much everyone had it in for the MacGregors – though to be fair they did rather bring it on themselves by constantly stealing everyone else's cattle, which must have been annoying.

Very often such feuds began with a casual or unthinking slight or what was taken as a slight. From then on, things had a habit of escalating fast. On Monday, a man from Clan X would be adjudged to have glanced 'with something akin to mild askancity' at the ghillie brogues of a man from Clan Y. By Wednesday, the mutual dissing would have reached fever pitch, accompanied by a couple of test kidnappings. By Friday, a great quantity of heads from both sides would have been hacked clear of their owners' shoulders to be made into

rafts and sailed in a full-scale assault on the enemy's crannogs. And it was all great fun until someone really got hurt. It's true what they say: … and ye shall ken the Highlands by the trail of dead.

And so we come to address the sad and terrible tale of the vicious feud between the MacLeods and the MacDonalds of Clanranald. There are several theories as to how the falling out began. The one that has gained most traction concerns itself with a visit to Eigg paid by some male MacLeods in 1577. The menfolk

of Eigg, all Clanranalds, were away from the island at the time and the MacLeods took the opportunity either to rape some of the women or attempt to take one or more away to force them into marriage. However, the MacDonalds happened to return while the MacLeods were still there. They tied the offending individuals up, put them back in their boats and set them adrift to meet an uncertain fate. The trussed-up sailors got lucky in that they were spotted and rescued by fellow clansmen who happened to be at sea.

To avenge themselves of this perceived ill-treatment, a large contingent of MacLeods made for Eigg. Seeing them coming and fearing the worst, the entire population of the island took refuge in a cave. It was called *Uamh Fhraing* ('Frances' Cave') and had a small entrance that was easily camouflaged. The MacLeods spent a good deal of time – perhaps several days – combing Eigg for its vanished inhabitants but eventually gave up

The smoke blew into the cave, suffocating everyone inside. The death toll ran to nearly 400

and sailed away. Unfortunately, it was at this point that one of those in the cave slipped out to check that the foe had gone. He was seen from the departing galleys and the secret of the cave was out.

The MacLeods returned and laid siege to *Uamh Fhraing*. The hiding place had become a trap. When the MacDonalds showed no sign of crawling out to face instant death by the sword, the invaders lit a big fire by the entrance. The smoke blew into the cave, suffocating everyone inside. The death toll ran to nearly 400.

It may have the ring of legend to it but, sadly, the massacre almost certainly happened. Corroborating evidence was supplied by sailor and author Hugh Miller who visited the cave in the 1840s. In his book *The Cruise of the Betsey*, Miller writes poignantly of the human bones he found inside. Those of adults and children were in little groups as if parents had gathered their offspring to them as the end came. Domestic objects were scattered about among the remains of straw mattresses.

From time to time bones are still unearthed in the cave, most recently in 2017. These grisly discoveries prompt rare visits to Eigg by the police, who otherwise do not have to trouble themselves with what is pretty much a crime-free island. Forensic tests on the bones have dated them back to the period of the massacre.

The journey the police make from the mainland to Eigg is one of the most picturesque in Britain. The island is 7 miles off the west coast of Scotland, one of the four main Small Isles – Eigg, Rum (pictured below, from Eigg), Canna and Muck – which are accessible by ferry from Mallaig. Eigg is the furthest east of this cluster and is easily recognisable by its one dramatic peak, An Sgurr, the largest pitchstone ridge in all of Europe.

The community that lives on the island today is thriving. As part of the Isle of Eigg Heritage Trust, the population of around 100 purchased their 12-square-mile island home from an absentee landlord in 1997. Since then they've become completely self-sufficient in renewable electricity, thanks to a system that combines

wind, solar and hydro power. It's the only such scheme in the world and the inhabitants are justly proud of it.

The Massacre Cave is on the south side of the island and is simple enough to find. From the pier, you pass the island's only shop and café-cum-pub to reach a woodside track. Where the track turns sharp left, you pick up a trail that is marked with occasional posts daubed with red paint. This is the Caves Walk, which takes visitors on a fairly flat grassy route before dropping sharply to the shore and the entrance to the Massacre Cave. There's a big map showing all eight waymarked island walks on a noticeboard near the pier, so take a photo as you pass it and you can't get lost.

What greets you down near the waves is a high but very narrow mouth to the cave which seems to come to an abrupt halt just a handful of yards in. It's only when you look down that you notice a small tunnel, just big enough to crawl through. Thoughtfully, there are a couple of builders-style safety hats left near the entrance for visitors to don. Once you have scrambled through the constricted aperture, the cave opens out. It extends a fair way back into the cliffside but must have been very cramped, noxious and generally disagreeable with nearly 400 people huddled together in there for what may have been days. With no other exit or air hole, it's all too easy to see how its occupants could have been asphyxiated by the incoming smoke.

Wiping out the entire population of the island didn't put an end to the feud. Members of Clanranald outwith Eigg bided their time and then, one Sunday some months later, they sailed in several boats from South Uist to Trumpan, near the northern tip of the Isle of Skye. A large party of MacLeods were attending a Sabbath service there and, crucially, the men were unarmed – one did not take a weapon into a holy place such as a kirk. The MacDonalds knew this, of course, and had timed their arrival accordingly. There was only one way out – a narrow door – and the MacDonalds readied their claymores – double-edged broadswords – to ensure no one left alive by that exit. They then set fire to the church, mockingly playing a tune on the pipes to accompany the screams of the men, women and children inside.

Alerted to what was happening by the column of smoke, a force of MacLeods raced up from Dunvegan. They engaged the men of Clanranald in a bloody affray but were too late to save those inside the church. More lives were lost on both sides in the skirmish, with just a few MacDonalds escaping in a single boat. 'War – what is it good for?' as Edwin Starr so rightly intoned.

If a visit to the Massacre Cave leaves you feeling a tad forlorn, there is another, much more substantial cave with slightly happier resonances just a short walk away along the coast.

The Cathedral Cave, which is only accessible at low tide, is where the island's inhabitants used to gather for Mass of a Sunday. Having been subject to persecution in the late 17th century on account of their Catholic faith, they were obliged to worship in secret to avoid further reprisals. This cave thus served as a conveniently discreet kirk.

Useful information

Always open | Admission free – likewise the Cathedral Cave (which is accessible at low tide only)
NB You'll need a torch to explore the Massacre Cave.

Getting there by public transport

Make your way to Mallaig, the terminus of the West Highland line. From there a Caledonian MacBrayne ferry (calmac.co.uk; 0800 066 5000) sails to the island several days a week in winter and every day in summer. From the pier, the directions to the Massacre Cave are as described in the main text on page 286. You'll find a stack of useful information on accommodation and getting about at isleofeigg.net

55

Tiny River
River Morar, Highlands

The River Bain (see page 157), diminutive though it may be, is positively Amazonian when compared with the River Morar. Scotland's shortest river with a name glides for just 800yd from its genesis at the northwestern tip of Loch Morar to the dramatic rapids that mark its end at the estuary of Morar Bay.

Only if you extend the putative length of the Morar to the low-tide mark of the sea near Sgeir Mhòr does the river attain any sort of grandeur at all. When Morar Bay empties and a residual channel of water can be seen snaking over the sands, the river could be said to measure about 2½ miles in total, equalling the extent of the Bain. But no one in their right mind would seek to do that, especially since the Morar makes up for its lack of stature in so many other ways.

It starts its odyssey as the outflow of one of Scotland's more extraordinary lochs. It's a surprisingly little-known fact that Loch Morar is the deepest loch in Scotland and indeed the deepest body of freshwater in Britain. At one point the loch bed is a cool 1,017ft below the surface, 262ft deeper than Loch Ness. Extreme profundity is not the only feature it shares with its more famous cousin: Loch Morar also lays claim to a monster.

'Mòrag', as the possibly legendary creature is known, has been reputedly sighted over 30 times since 1887. By far the most thrilling encounter occurred in 1969. According to the Loch Ness Investigation's annual report of that year, two long-distance lorry drivers, William Simpson (22) and Duncan McDonell (35), actually claimed to have been in some sort of fisticuffs situation with Mòrag on the evening

of 16 August. The two friends were heading north across the loch in Simpson's cabin cruiser towards the village of Morar, not far from where the River Morar drains the loch. They felt a bump, having given an inadvertent glancing blow to something below the waterline. Immediately following the collision, Simpson went below to see to a kettle that had been knocked off a gas ring. Alerted by shouts from McDonell, he went back up on deck to find his friend battling with Mòrag. The oar McDonell had been using as a weapon had already been broken in two in the fracas. Simpson grabbed his .22 rifle and fired. The creature quickly slipped beneath the waves, although Simpson stated that he did not know whether he had hit it or not. The two men gave separate television news interviews soon afterwards in which they both appeared shaken by their experience. The stories they told of the encounter tallied with each other.

Leaving the loch and its potentially scarred inhabitant, the River Morar heads more or less south. A row of jetties, home to myriad day boats, crowds the tree-lined western bank before the river takes a sharp turn west towards the sea and, more immediately, a weir and a fish ladder. In common with its diminutive English cousin, the River Morar powers a hydroelectric plant, which was installed at this point back in 1948.

Curiously, for a waterway so short, the Morar has two crossings. A viaduct built in 1897 takes the railway line high above the waters towards its terminus at Mallaig, a few miles to the north. An elegant construction, the viaduct is now a listed building. Right next to it, but considerably lower, is the rather less comely bridge carrying the B8008 into the village of Morar. This used to be the A830, part of the Road to the Isles from Fort William to Mallaig, until a new, larger main road was opened in 1997, providing the village of Morar with a bypass and Morar Bay with its very first crossing. At the river's

Scotland's shortest river with a name glides for just 800yd from its genesis at the northwestern tip of Loch Morar

end, just to the west of the B8008 bridge, the Morar takes a great lurch downwards towards the estuary. The place is sometimes known as the Falls of Morar, although the Rapids of Morar would be a more accurate description. The scant remains of an earlier Road to the Isles bridge can be seen here at the last point where the waterway is narrow enough to allow an easy crossing. This steep rock step also marks the high point of the tide, ensuring that Loch Morar is not tainted with salt water.

To the west lies the estuary of Morar Bay and the northern end of the Silver Sands of Morar. The white sand that gives the beaches their name is quite spectacular. On a sunny day it feels as if you have been transported far to the south and that the islands of Eigg and Rum across the Sound of Sleat must be Greek isles floating in the Aegean.

However, things weren't so peaceful here back in 1602. The Battle of Morar was fought in the vicinity that year as the climax to yet another feud between Scottish clans. In this case it was the Mackenzies and the MacDonells who had fallen out, with the predictable litany of murders and other crimes perpetrated by both sides. Details of the encounter are sketchy, but it appears that men from Clan Ross also made an appearance, fighting on the side of the Mackenzies, with whom they were linked by marriage. There was apparently great loss of life on both sides and no clear winner, although some sort of peace was brokered afterwards, which is a better outcome than was usual in such affairs.

Today, aside from acting as a picturesque umbilical cord between Loch Morar and the sea, the River Morar also performs a useful ecclesiastical function. It provides a boundary between the palindromic parish of Glenelg (to the north) and the more conventionally named parish of Arisaig and Moidart (to the south). It is surely more than coincidence that, all the while the Morar has flowed from loch to sea, these two parishes have never gone to war with each other.

Getting there by public transport

Morar railway station, towards the northern end of the notoriously scenic West Highland line, is just half a mile away along the B8008.

Tiny Camera Obscura
The Hut of the Shadow, Western Isles

In a world where we don't give a second thought to the fact that someone in Reykjavik can live-stream images of their cat doing something amusing with kelp to an appreciative audience in Western Samoa, it's a curious thing that camerae obscurae still have any appeal left at all.

And yet the camera obscura on the Royal Mile in Edinburgh is still one of the Scottish capital's major attractions, while others continue to thrive (or at least continue) in Bristol, Portslade, Kirriemuir, Chester, Aberystwyth, Todmorden, Greenwich, Portmeirion, Dumfries and the Isles of Scilly to name but a few.

And to that list we can add a rather obscurer obscura. On a headland barely worth the name, near the village of Lochmaddy on the island of North Uist in the Western Isles, far out into the Atlantic Ocean, sits a very unobtrusive stone hut. Any stray tourists who pass this way – and they're few and far between – would

be forgiven for imagining that it's a squat Neolithic dwelling, or a replica of one. After all, there's a 5,000-year-old burial chamber just down the road. But inside is one of North Uist's more surprising finds.

The island of North Uist is at the northern end of the southern half of the Western Isles. It's home to Europe's largest breeding colony of common and Atlantic grey seals and some of the Outer Hebrides' highest peaks. From the summit of the Eabhal it's possible to see the remote island group of St Kilda when the weather allows.

But when the weather does not allow, there's the Hut of the Shadow.

Part of the Uist Sculpture Trail, it was designed by Chris Drury and mimics a Neolithic stone tumulus. It has a grass roof which, in combination with the stone walls that match the outcropping rocks around them, goes some way to disguising the presence of the building, thus adding to its mystique. A picket gate protects the entrance. Inside, a curved passage takes visitors rapidly into a small chamber. Here there are three mirrors built into a wall which, with the aid of a lens, between them form a camera obscura (Latin for 'dark room') projecting an image of Loch nam Madadh onto the opposite wall. The better the light is outside, the higher the quality of the image that forms inside the hut. If you time it right you might find yourself watching a boat putter past or a flock of birds land on the water.

When you leave though, do close the gate behind you because otherwise the hut is likely to fill with sheep – and like any camera obscura it works best if you keep it clean.

Camerae obscurae, in one form or another, may well have been with us for thousands or even tens of thousands of years. Some archaeologists believe that the distended animals seen in many Palaeolithic cave paintings may have been inspired by images that were inadvertently projected by light passing through tiny holes in the pelt roofs of shelters. It makes the siting of one in a Neolithic-style structure suddenly rather less outré.

The first written record of the form of camera obscura we know today was penned by Leonardo da Vinci in a notebook he kept in 1502. It was very much later, in the 19th century, that they had their heyday in Britain. They became almost a staple of seaside resorts where holidaymakers would flock to them to stand amazed at the spectacle of a picture that moved.

The Hut of the Shadow offers a much more private and personal experience than the camerae

Any stray tourists who pass this way – and they're few and far between – would be forgiven for imagining that it's a squat Neolithic dwelling obscurae of old or the ones that keep the flame today. On a sunny day, as the light hits the wall, flickering in time with the eddies of the loch, it almost feels like you're bathing in the waters that ripple outside.

Useful information

Near Lochmaddy | Always open | Admission free

Getting there by public transport

The Western Isles (sometimes known as the Outer Hebrides) are somewhat off the beaten track but the effort repays itself many times over. Take the train to the Kyle of Lochalsh, the terminus of the hauntingly beautiful Kyle of Lochalsh line. From the harbour jump on the 915 or 916 coach (www.citylink.co.uk; 0141 332 9644) to Uig on the Isle of Skye via the Skye Bridge. From the ferry terminal at Uig board a vessel over the Minch to Lochmaddy on North Uist (calmac.co.uk; 0800 066 5000)

The Hut of the Shadow is located at Sponàis/Sponish, which is just over a mile from the pier at Lochmaddy. Head up the main road (A865), taking the first right after about 700yd. Follow this to a crossroads, heading straight over, passing a police station and an outdoor activity centre. The road becomes a track leading to a suspension footbridge. (At the time of going to press the footbridge was closed but it should be open in 2018. If not, the only alternative is a yomp along the A865 out of the village until you reach the first track on the right – this will lead back more or less all the way to the other end of the footbridge.) All being well, from the footbridge you'll see the Hut of the Shadow on a headland to your right.

NB The HS6 5AE postcode sometimes quoted for the hut will not take you out of Lochmaddy.

57

Tiny Ferry
Cape Wrath Ferry, Sutherland

Take away the fact that they both have lighthouses and the far northern corners of mainland Britain are contrasting affairs. Duncansby Head, the most northeasterly point, has John O'Groats just down the road with its postcards, memorabilia, sensationally unprepossessing hotel and a constant stream of cyclists and motorbikers rolling in fresh from Land's End.

Cape Wrath, on the other hand, has precisely nowhere for a neighbour and almost seems to pride itself on its isolation. It's accessible only via a tortuous pathless tramp north along the west coast from the nearest road 12 miles away, or by paying the plain-speaking John Morrison to ferry you across the ever-shifting channels of the Kyle of Durness in his tiny craft.

The Kyle is a wide coastal inlet that slashes down into this northern coastline for over 5 miles, carving a great big scar the shape of an elongated 'S'. It effectively cuts off the Cape Wrath peninsula from the land to the east. The variation in the tides is

such that at the lowest ebb there's only one viable place where the ferry can sail from shore to shore. At Keoldale, 2 miles south of the coast, the channel fortuitously lurches across the sands from the west bank to the east.

Even so, the ferryman's craft is necessarily tiny, for only a vessel with a very shallow draught can cross the Kyle at low tide when sand banks abound and grounding becomes a very real possibility for larger vessels. The boat has an outboard motor, a bright blue hull and an open-ended cabin that gives shelter on cold or wet days to the lucky few who board first. Greeting them on the far side of the Kyle is a wilderness through which no roads run. However, there is a minibus that will take you on a track to the cape across 11 miles of land so inhospitable that the Ministry of Defence has taken to bombing it from both air and sea. It's apparently unique in being the only firing range in the UK onto which aircraft can drop 1,000lb bombs.

The only other way of getting to Cape Wrath is to tramp along the track from the ferry landing over an undulating treeless terrain.

The 'wrath' of Cape Wrath is derived from the Old Norse word *hvarf* meaning 'turning point'. However, it might as well have taken its name from the ferocious Atlantic seas that boil below the gargantuan cliffs. They're whipped up by the gale force winds that pummel the place every 10 days on average. The lighthouse, designed by Robert Stevenson, was built in 1828 in a largely successful attempt to stem the flow of shipwrecks that occurred beneath this towering rockface.

Back in the 1930s, the peninsula was populated, albeit sparsely.

The ferryman's craft is necessarily tiny, for only a vessel with a very shallow draught can cross the Kyle at low tide

Around 35 people scratched a living here, mainly from crofting. Now the only inhabitants are John and Kay Ure who live in the former lighthouse keepers' cottage. They run the Ozone Café from the lighthouse, an eatery famous for claiming that it is open 365 days a year, 24 hours a day (though it might not do any harm to give them a ring ahead if you're planning to rock up at three in the morning).

Every May, the ferry plays a possibly unique role: it becomes an essential part of a long-distance race. The gruelling Cape Wrath Marathon, the climax to a week of running events called the Cape Wrath Challenge, is reckoned to be one of the toughest marathons in Britain, and includes ascents totalling nearly 2,500ft. The race starts extremely early (at 5.45am for some competitors) with a bus and ferry ride across to the Kyle to the start point on the far shore, a spot called Capeside. Having hauled themselves over to the Cape Wrath lighthouse and back, runners may well find themselves cooling their heels in a queue while the little ferry shuttles their fellows across the river a dozen or so at a time. After a punishing 22 miles, with leg muscles tightening up, the agony of waiting for the boat must be exquisite indeed.

At least the officials do everyone the kindness of stopping the clocks once they reach Capeside, only starting them again when the ferry has landed them safely at Keoldale…where a final punishing climb into Durness awaits.

The village that acts as a finish line is a pleasant though rather stretched-out affair. The British mainland's most northwesterly settlement contains all the amenities a visitor might require, including a convenience store, a variety of accommodation (including a campsite and hostel), a pub and, at Faraid Head, plentiful puffins to watch. It also possesses a (somewhat forlorn) memorial garden dedicated to the

first Beatle to leave us. John Lennon's song *In My Life* is believed to have been inspired by the many happy childhood holidays he spent with an aunt and uncle who lived in a crofters' cottage close by.

Useful information

Cape Wrath Ferry: Sailings every day from May–Sep | Adult return £7, adult single £5, child return £5 | capewrathferry.wordpress.com
01971 511246 / 07719 678729

Cape Wrath Minibus: Two or three trips daily from early Apr–mid-Oct (weather, MoD and demand permitting) | Adult return £12, adult single £7, child return £7 (cash only) | visitcapewrath.com
01971 511284 / 07742 670196

Ozone Café: Serving hot and cold snacks, drinks and souvenirs | Always open | 01971 511314

Cape Wrath Challenge: Book your marathon place well in advance because numbers are limited | capewrathchallenge.co.uk

Getting there by public transport

Understandably, unless you happen to be in the fortunate position of living nearby, it takes some time to get to the most northwesterly village on the British mainland and within striking distance of the Cape Wrath Ferry. However, it can be done and with relative ease if you take a train first to northern Scotland and don't want to travel on a Sunday.

On weekdays simply get yourself to Lairg railway station for the 806 bus which runs once a day at just after midday or the 804 bus at 3.50pm (also at this time on Saturday); every Saturday the 803 bus runs along the north coast from near Thurso railway station to Durness while the 805 bus starts its journey from Inverness, going via Lairg (all buses thedurnessbus.com; 01971 511223 / 07782 110007). Bicycles can be carried on the 804 and 806 but must be booked at least a day in advance.

58

Tiny Street
Ebenezer Place, Caithness

Wick is one of the more remote places on the British mainland, tucked away on the far northeast coast of Scotland. As the crow flies the town is 415 miles from Birmingham and 580 miles from Penzance. Even Edinburgh is 170 miles away. To put it into context, these flights are all way too far for any crow to contemplate, given their habit of travelling a maximum of 40 miles from their daytime feeding areas to their night-time roost sites.

If you don't happen to be in Caithness, Wick (*Inbhir Ùige* in Gaelic) may feel like quite a long way to go to see a very short street (even if it is recognised not only as the shortest street in Britain but the shortest on the entire planet). However, this is tempered by the fact that not only can you buy a drink there, you can also eat there, dance there and even stay the night there. When one considers that the street in question is just 6ft 9in long – the length of Stephen Fry balancing a hardback copy of *Don Quixote* on his head – then that's not altogether shabby.

The position of the street is rather unusual. It's at the meeting of five other roads – Cliff Road, Station Road, Bridge Street, Union Street and River Street – which come together like unevenly placed spokes in a wheel. If you imagine a hub in the centre of that wheel, where all the spokes join together, Ebenezer Place is a little section of that hub separating the spokes of Union Street and River Street. The river referred to by the latter is the River Wick, which passes through the town and flows into the sea through its harbour. Bridge Street passes over the Bridge of Wick, one

of a pair of crossings that keep the two sides of the town joined up.

Some might suggest that there really isn't a need to recognise this tiny stretch of Wick's transport infrastructure as a street at all. The town's good councillors evidently disagreed when Alexander Sinclair returned to his home town a rich man after doing rather well in the United States and built a hotel here in 1883. Wedged in between River Street and Union Street, it had entrances onto both but also had a very short side facing directly onto the five-roads junction. The council deemed it necessary for this side of the building to have a proper street address and so Ebenezer Place was born. Sinclair was pressed into advertising the street name on the building and four years later both the street and its name were officially recognised in the town's records. If you go there today and look up you can still see the original 'Ebenezer Place' tympanum high

> The street in question is just 6ft 9in long – the length of Stephen Fry balancing a hardback copy of *Don Quixote* on his head

up on the gable end of Mackays Hotel, underneath an imposing chimney stack.

The council being no nest of small-town tyrants, Sinclair was allowed to choose the name for the street. He heroically eschewed the opportunity to call it Alexander Sinclair Street or Stop Wasting My Time With Your Pettifogging Requests Boulevard. The reasoning behind his selection of 'Place' is obvious enough, since that term is usually applied to a square or a short street. The 'Ebenezer' part is a little more obscure. Today, the association most likely to come to mind is with Ebenezer Scrooge, the miser from Charles Dickens' 1843 classic novella *A Christmas Carol*. The connection would have been made in 1883 as well, of course. However, those were the days when the average citizen was much more versed in the Bible, and Sinclair may well have been referencing the original Eben-Ezer, which appears in the Old Testament. It means 'stone of help' and was erected by a Hebrew prophet called Samuel in thanks for his god Jehovah's help in overcoming the Philistine army in a battle at Aphek, by the western entrance of the pass of Beth-Horon. In settling on the name, perhaps Sinclair felt he was offering a similar nod of appreciation to the Divine Being for assistance in accruing his fortune in the States.

Whatever the background to the name, to all intents and purposes the street itself 'disappeared' for a long period. When Guinness World Records went looking for the shortest street in the world, they happened upon Elgin Street in Bacup, Lancashire, which held the title for many years. That thoroughfare is a hulking great 17ft long and no one in their right mind wants to walk that far, so it was a relief when Mackays Hotel decided to open up a door to their bistro on the one side of the establishment that lacked an entrance. This was enough for the adjudicators at Guinness World Records to declare Ebenezer Place a bona fide street because it now contained a building with an address: No. 1 Bistro, Ebenezer Place. And so in 2006 the record passed north of the border.

Useful information

Mackays Hotel: Home of the No. 1 Bistro, the only address on Ebenezer Place, KW1 5ED
Open daily noon–5pm for lunch and 5–9pm for dinner
mackayshotel.co.uk | 01955 602323

Getting there by public transport

Wick may be one of the more remote places on the British mainland, but it does have a railway station. Wick is one of the two termini of the evocatively named Far North line (along with Thurso, Britain's most northerly station). Indeed, since all trains travelling north first call at Thurso before reversing to Georgemas Junction and heading to Wick, it is the operational terminus of the line. From the station, it's less than 200yd away – head along Station Road until it arrives at the five-way junction. Ebenezer Street is straight in front of you, between River Street and Union Street.

Tiny Island
Eynhallow, Orkney

Of all the islands that make up the wonderful exploding jigsaw puzzle that is Orkney, Eynhallow is the real trickster, the joker, the one that refuses to be bound by the everyday rules governing what we perceive to be reality. Its role in Norse mythology is far more important than its history – and what history it does have reads like magical realism.

A dollop of land in Eynhallow Sound, the swiftly rushing channel that separates Mainland Orkney from the isle of Rousay, Eynhallow superficially appears similar to many another tiny uninhabited Scottish island. It's a treeless place, open and apparently desolate but for seabirds – 185 acres of grass and rocky fringes, rising gradually to a summit, if that is not too ambitious a word for it, that is just 130ft above the waves. There's not a road nor a path to guide the traveller or to show that people once lived here. The only sign of possible habitation can be found near the southeastern shore where there squats

the single-storey Eynhallow Bothy. This sizeable hut is used occasionally by students coming to the island to monitor the bird population. Naturally, there is no ferry service.

It must be said that Eynhallow is unusual in that a legend of invisibility has attached itself to the isle. Sailors were reputed to have reported that it sometimes simply vanished before their eyes as they approached it. However, there are several Scottish islands that are believed to be able to carry off that trick (as well as some further afield, such as the Isle of Man). And like many a wild and apparently inhospitable Scottish

isle, Eynhallow is home to a ruined church. But here it does score over its fellows, for Eynhallow has a church that disappeared for hundreds of years and then reappeared.

The story bids us go back in time to the 12th century. Or possibly earlier. Or maybe a little later – nobody can be sure. It was sometime in that period of the Middle Ages that a Norse monastery was founded on the island. Or if not a Norse monastery, at least some sort of Norse monastic outpost. There are no written records to indicate exactly what was founded on the island. However, we

do know that the name Eynhallow
is a corruption of the Old Norse
Eyin-Helga which means 'Holy Isle', a
name sometimes used for the island.
And we also know that some of the
remains of the church date back to
sometime in the 12th century, give or
take 50 years either way, probably.

Whenever it was built, the church
or the monastery was probably
abandoned at the time of the
Reformation in the 16th century.
At some point shortly after this
occurred, a thrifty person in need
of accommodation on the island
decided to use the church as the

basis for a house and adapted it into a two-storey residence. At least two further dwellings were built next door and roofed with thatch. The families who lived there no doubt scraped a meagre living from the sea and from livestock grazed on the island. Over time, the previous life of one of the houses was forgotten.

In 1851, when the hamlet on Eynhallow ran to four families, an unwelcome visitor arrived. Some sort of deadly disease – again, it's not clear what but it might have been typhoid contracted via water from the island's well – began to strike down the inhabitants. The whole population of the island was forced to flee. There has been no permanent human presence ever since. As a precaution against others coming and living (and probably shortly thereafter dying) in the abandoned homes, their roofs were removed. It was only then, with the conversion work laid bare, that it was realised that one of the houses must once have been a church.

According to Historic Environment Scotland, in whose care Eynhallow

It is a treeless place, open and apparently desolate but for seabirds – 185 acres of grass and rocky fringes

Church rests, the church may once have consisted of a nave with a porch to the west and a chancel (which contained the altar) at its eastern end. Although most of the extensive ruins that can be seen today are of the 16th-century house, it's still possible to make out the nave's gabled ends and parts of the porch and chancel walls. The grass-topped walls of the ruins, complete with Romanesque arches inside and monumental buttresses to shore up the building against the gales, are fascinating to look at close up. Budding archaeological detectives can try their hand at discerning what is 16th-century house and what is very much older church. They can also puzzle over the small blocks of partially dressed red sandstone that lie about in the ruins of an outhouse. These must have been imported to the island and look suspiciously similar to the type of stones used in St Magnus Cathedral in Kirkwall on Orkney Mainland.

Were they ever used as part of the church or monastery, and, if so, to what purpose? Were they removed by whoever converted the building into a house? The truth has yet to be uncovered.

The remnants of two other houses next to the church can also be viewed for a sobering insight into just how austere life must have been for those who lived within their cramped walls.

So much for the actual history of the Holy Isle. Its other soubriquet, gained on account of yet more Norse influence, is the Enchanted Isle. Eynhallow, it turns out, used to be the summer home of the Finfolk. It would still be so today but for a terrible trick that was played on them by a wily farmer. They can hardly complain though because they themselves were always up to artful dodges.

The Finfolk were a peculiarly Orcadian phenomenon. They were an amphibious race of rather shadowy and glum peripatetic shape-shifting sorcerers who were excellent sailors and just as at home on land as they were at the bottom of the sea. Understandably, humans were rather wary of them. They left Orkney each year to spend the winter at Finfolkaheem, an apparently idyllic city whose whereabouts were a secret. Each summer they would come back to Orkney, where they would cause all sorts of grief. Their favourite occupation was the abduction of the locals. The victims would be spirited away to some distant island to be married to a Finman or a Finwife, neither of whom are said to have made particularly agreeable spouses. One imagines that such kidnappings often took place when storms raged and there were fishermen out at sea in flimsy craft.

The Finfolk's base of operations in Orkney was Hildaland, and it was on this island that the trick played on them took place. They had it coming to them really. The wife of a man named Thorodale, who lived with their three sons in the parish of Evie on Mainland Orkney, was one day captured by a Finman. He dragged her into his boat. Thorodale, alerted by his wife's screams, gave chase in his own vessel. Then in an instant the Finman, his victim and his boat all disappeared. Thorodale declared that he would get his wife back and avenge himself on the Finfolk. One day, while fishing in Eynhallow Sound, he heard the voice of his wife singing a song in which she advised him to seek out the wise woman who lived on the island of Hoy.

She told our hero how he could see the invisible island of Hildaland. This involved him traipsing out to the Odin Stone of Stenness at midnight on the nights of nine consecutive full moons. On each occasion he would get down on his knees and circle the stone nine times. This worked, of course, and when he saw Hildaland he asked his three sons to accompany him there in a boat weighed down by a prodigious cargo of salt.

The journey involved several dramatic incidents including attacks by whales, the lascivious attentions of mermaids, an assault by a monster and finally the swordplay of the very Finman who had kidnapped Thorodale's wife. These foes were each in turn overcome by the judicious throwing of salt – which was seen as a holy cleanser – or crosses made out of grasses. Thorodale then ordered his sons to go about the island scattering the remaining salt in nine circles. The Finfolk fled in terror, never to be seen there again. Thorodale renamed the isle Eynhallow, which, in its newly sanctified state, remained visible. He never did get his wife back though.

Despite this ejection of the Finfolk from their summer home, it was only in the 19th century that the belief in the dark shape-shifting fiends finally faded away. Which sounds like no bad thing really.

Getting there by public transport

There are only two ways of reaching Eynhallow. You can charter a boat from Rousay or (more easily) Orkney Mainland – the iCentre in West Castle Street, Kirkwall, Orkney Mainland can help with this (01856 872856). Or you can time it right (and book well in advance) and join the evening trip to the island undertaken by Orkney Heritage Society (orkneycommunities.co.uk/ohs) every July.

Orkney Ferries run frequent scheduled services to Rousay from Tingwall on Orkney Mainland all year round (orkneyferries.co.uk | 01856 872044)

Tiny Cinema
Schoolhouse Cinema, Shetland

Not only is this the smallest cinema in Scotland but it must surely have one of the most meagre potential audiences of any cinema on the planet. The little archipelago of Out Skerries, off the east coast of Shetland Mainland, has two inhabited islands whose combined population as recorded by the most recent census was just 74.

It's probably as well that the owner – magician, entertainer and firebreather Chris Harris – does not intend the cinema to be a money-spinner. Indeed, not only is entry free to his 20-seat palace of film, which he opened in 2017, but the popcorn, hotdogs, Slush Puppies, drinks and snacks are all on the house too.

Englishman Harris moved to the Out Skerries in 2016 and took up residence in the rambling former schoolhouse. A long-standing fan of film, he had a collection of 4,000 DVDs, a red velvet curtain (doubtless the sort of thing you do own if you're a magician) and a projector,

so the decision to open a cinema came naturally.

In an interview with the *Shetland Times*, he said: 'When I bought the Schoolhouse, I realised quite early on it was a big house and I thought it would be a shame having just room after room.'

Despite being based in his own home, there's no denying that the cinema offers the full authentic picture-house

experience. The auditorium's big blue comfortable seats made the long and difficult journey up to their new island home from an Odeon in Manchester. There's a popcorn machine, Dolby surround sound, an outsize Oscar statuette bearing the cinema's name and proper tickets proudly printed 'Out Skerries – Cinema Ticket – Admit One'. In January 2018, the innovative owner even added a bijou spa and mini gym to his tiny empire.

The islands now served by the cinema are low-lying, windswept and possessed of an understated beauty. They have been inhabited since the Neolithic era, were invaded and colonised by Norse folk, and even played a role in World War II, acting as a convenient landing point for refugees escaping from Norway, 200 miles away across the North Sea.

You've got to take your hat off to Harris – not only is he providing a cinema where no cinema might ever have been imagined to take root but, being the showman that he is, he could easily have installed 18 seats instead of 20 and claimed the title of Smallest Cinema in the UK. He told the *Shetland Times*: 'I've always found in life when things are getting a bit hard there's nothing like going to the cinema and escaping; even if it's an hour-and-a-half or two hours of escapism, it's something for the soul.'

All power to his popcorn.

Useful information

Films selected and shown on an informal basis – have a chat with Chris Harris when you make it to the islands
Admission free | schoolhousecinema.co.uk

Getting there by public transport

Despite its remoteness, Out Skerries is comparatively simple to get to. A ferry (shetland.gov.uk/ferries; 01595 693535) sails from Lerwick and Vidlin, both on Shetland Mainland. To reach the latter from Lerwick, take the thrice-daily number 19 bus (leaskstravel.co.uk; 01595 693162). The sailing from Lerwick takes approximately 2½ hours and it's 1½ hours from Vidlin. If there are fierce northerly winds blowing, the ferry sails from Laxo, a little to the north of Vidlin (also served by the 19). There is bed and breakfast accommodation available on Out Skerries and a couple of shops selling groceries. The two inhabited Skerries islands, Housay and Bruray, are linked by a bridge. The ferry comes into Bruray, the more easterly of the two low-lying islands, and it's about a 10-minute walk to the Schoolhouse on Housay (or West Isle, as it is known to locals).

Author's Acknowledgements

No man is an island, and rarely is a book a solo effort. This one certainly wasn't and I'd like to thank all those who aided me in big ways and small. It's very much appreciated, even though it may not have seemed that way when I heartlessly guffawed at the more hare-brained suggestions that came my way (tiny bus stops, anyone?) The following individuals were free with their time and skills and I'm grateful to you all:

Klur Memphis Robertson (Scots adviser)
Flora and Spike Houston
Sophie Brandon
Lisa-Raine and Jackson, Rob and Laura, James and Rachel
Kelly Allnut
Geoff Lusher at Pre Metro Operations
Alex and Sue at Platform 3

Nothing gets the literary juices flowing quite like a scenic bolthole in which to write. I've been extremely fortunate in knowing a number of excellent types who let me hunker down with a laptop for extended periods of time in their well-appointed properties. Some, I suspect, are beginning to wonder if the only reason I write books nowadays is to have an excuse to do some freeloading. To be honest, it's probably best if we draw a discreet veil over that. Dans le meantime, I doff my cap to you all and thank you for being such fine and generous hosts:

The Boys
Debs and Neil
Kim and Nick
Mark, Jude, Seth and Silas
Michèle and Richard

Last, but not in the slightest bit least, are the folk who dedicate their lives to turning my deathless prose into the book you have in your hands right now.

There's Donna Wood, who saw everything onto the page and edited feverishly away, sometimes even securing permission from the author to cut a comma or ditch a diphthong. Judith Forshaw had the unenviable task of fact-checking and proofreading the whole thing to make sure not a single mistake made it into prunt.

James Tims and Tom Whitlock were in charge of the visual stuff that gives readers a pleasant rest from what might otherwise seem an unending flow of words. And there's Helen Brocklehurst who correctly divined that *Tiny Britain* was an idea worth making a reality. Do take a bow, one and all.

Perhaps if you're reading this now you could clap, otherwise they're going to feel ridiculous.

Picture Credits

AA Media wishes to thank the following illustrators, photographers and organisations for their assistance in the preparation of this book. Abbreviations for the picture credits are as follows – (t) top; (b) bottom; (l) left; (r) right; (c) centre

Mapping illustrations by David Wardle

Endpapers – Bucket & Spade and Snorkel & Mask: marco varrone/Alamy; Compass & Lamp: Artur Balytskyi/Alamy; Crown: Panther Media GmbH/Alamy; Football: Saint_A/Alamy; Lobster: Artspace/Alamy; Puppet: Sergey Pykhonin/Alamy; Seabird: Oleksandra Kukhar/ Alamy. 8 Artur Balytskyi/Alamy; 9t Dixe Wills; 13 David Chapman/Alamy; 14-15 Oleksandra Kukhar/Alamy; 16 way out west photography/Alamy; 20-21 Nature Photographers Ltd/Alamy; 26-27 Stephen Spraggon/Alamy; 30-31 Clive Fairchild; 36 Keith Ryan; 41 Stephen Mithan/ Alamy; 43 marco varrone/Alamy; 46 Adam Burton/Alamy; 52 Saint_A/Alamy; 55 Courtesy of Forest Green Rovers; 57 Courtesy of the Bournemouth Colosseum; 60 Greg Balfour Evans/ Alamy; 65 Dixe Wills; 70-71 Mark Beton/Metro/Alamy; 73 Panther Media GmbH/Alamy; 77 rod williams/Alamy; 80 Justin Kase z10z/Alamy; 85 Tony Watson/Alamy; 88-89 Rick Strange/ Alamy; 95 John Gaffen / Alamy; 100-101 Andrew Sharpe/Alamy; 105 M J Perris/Alamy; 108 John Worrall/Alamy; 114-115 Alistair Laming/Alamy; 118-119 Chris Herring/Alamy; 123 LH Images/Alamy; 125 Sergey Pykhonin/Alamy; 127 Martin Bond/Alamy; 129 JohanH/Alamy; 132-133 Gordon Bell/Alamy; 134 YAY Media AS/Alamy; 138 Jim Bell; 143 Warley Community Association in association with Chris and Paul Czainski.; 148-149 John Morrison/Alamy; 154-155 Realimage/Alamy; 158 Bethan Osman/Alamy; 159 curved-light/Alamy; 163 Jon Arnold Images Ltd/Alamy; 164 Artur Balytskyi/Alamy; 168-169 Ashley Cooper pics / Alamy; 176-177 Jorge Tutor/Alamy; 180 joan gravell/Alamy; 185 Christopher Nicholson/Alamy; 188-189 Stephen Sykes/Alamy; 191t marco varrone/Alamy; 191b marco varrone/Alamy; 195 David Angel/Alamy; 200-201 The Photolibrary Wales/Alamy; 202 Artur Balytskyi/Alamy; 206 Mark Zawisza; 210-211 Gavin Haskell/Alamy; 214 Tony Trasmundi/Alamy; 217 Jon March Photographics/Alamy; 220 Ian G Dagnall/Alamy; 227 Courtesy of The Swallow Theatre; 232-233 Kenny Williamson/Alamy; 236-237 National Museums of Scotland; 241 Duncan Astbury/ Alamy; 246-247 Clearview/Alamy; 249 Artspace/Alamy; 252-253 Ross Gilmore/Alamy; 254 Ross Gilmore/Alamy; 260-261 Doug Houghton SCO/Alamy; 267 Ian Paterson/Alamy; 270-271 Christina Bollen/Alamy; 276 Worldwide Picture Library/Alamy; 280 Sheila Halsall/Alamy; 284 Pete Marshall - Places/Alamy; 286 allan wright/Alamy; 290-291 Dennis Hardley/Alamy; 295 Andy Sutton/Alamy; 300-301 ScotImage/Alamy; 304 MARK HICKEN/Alamy; 308-309 Doug Houghton/Alamy; 313 Ingram Publishing/Alamy Stock Vector; 314 Courtesy of The Schoolhouse Cinema; 318-319 Dru Norris/Alamy.

Every effort has been made to trace the copyright holders, and we apologise in advance for any unintentional omissions or errors. We would be pleased to apply any corrections in a following edition of this publication.